Seed Bead
Stitching

Seed Bead
Stitching

Creative Variations on Traditional Techniques

Beth Stone

Dedication

For Cheyenne and Sierra, the art of my heart. And for Sheldon, with love.

www.Kalmbach.com/Books

Printed in the United States of America

14 13 12 11 10   6 7 8 9 10

8-22-16

Publisher's Cataloging-In-Publication Data

Stone, Beth, 1960–
  Seed bead stitching : creative variations on traditional techniques / Beth Stone.

  p. : ill. ; cm.

  ISBN: 978-0-87116-252-6

1. Beadwork—Handbooks, manuals, etc. 2. Beadwork—Patterns. 3. Jewelry making. I. Title.

TT860 .S76 2007
745.594/2

Contents

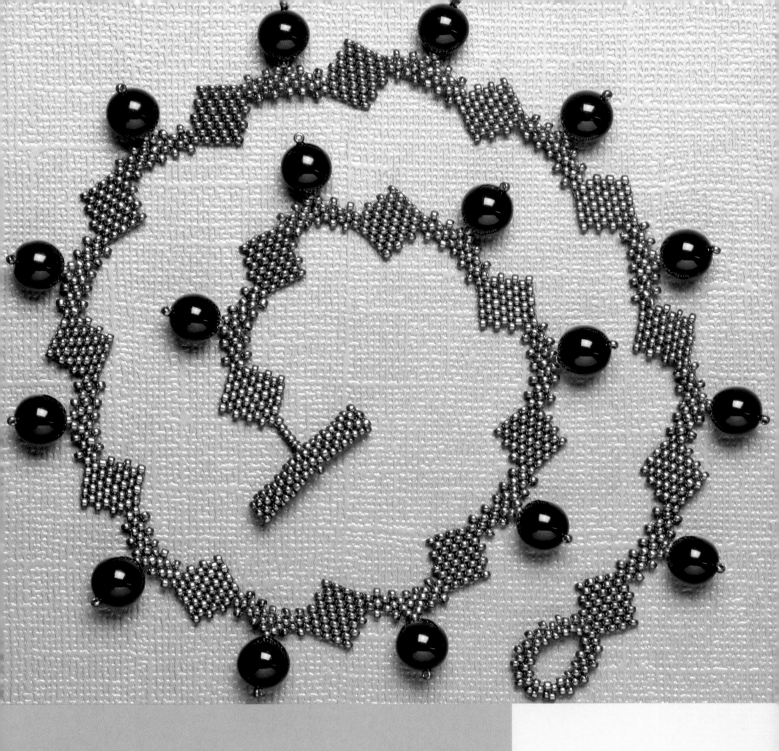

Introduction

All I really need are beads

One of my favorite bead class icebreakers is the question, "Beads or food?" Or, better yet, "Beads or chocolate?" After the initial laughter, there is some serious discussion about these questions. We all know we need food to live, but those of us who love beads need beads to survive. And much like chocolate, beads are addictive. We love to buy them, look at them, touch them, travel with them, show them off, covet them, and share them. We get so lost in our beads that sometimes we forget to eat, even chocolate. We can spend hours or days trying to figure out a stitch, trying to invent a stitch, or working out a new variation of a tried-and-true stitch. We'll spend hours in stores or on the Internet searching for that perfect color, size, texture, or combination. These tiny, shiny pieces of glass, stone, pearl, or metal make us forget about the rest of the world (as well as the husbands and loved ones we left on the bench outside of the bead store). There is something fascinating about beads, something difficult to describe but easy to understand once you enter the beading world.

Getting started

Where do we begin? As artists, we look for inspiration wherever we can find it. We look at nature, fabrics, paintings, and yes, even the work of other beaders. We love the "I wonder how to do that," the "I have to learn how to do that," and the "I love that color scheme" moments. We love to imagine something in our minds and to then have it slowly appear in our hands. While there is much discussion about copying the work of others, there is a definite line between learning from other artists and profiting from their work. If we don't share what we know and love, we can't inspire and teach. The art cannot continue if we hide our work. I thank the artists who have generously shared their work before me and I thank those who will share their work — perhaps from something they learn here — after me. I believe that with the knowledge of musical notes, you can write a song. With the knowledge of 26 letters, you can write a story. And with the knowledge of a few basic bead-stitching techniques, you can create a piece of beaded art.

In this book, you will find the basics of many traditional beading stitches, as well as fun and interesting variations of these stitches. I hope you will take what you learn and find the confidence to make it your own, to find your own beading "voice." Even intermediate and advanced beaders may learn a new stitch or two, or may simply find a new or unexpected way to use or combine stitches. No matter what your skill level is, you'll find that many of the ideas and projects presented here can be completed quickly – in hours as opposed to days. The design possibilities are as unlimited as your imagination. Use colors and textures that you like. Combine stitches in ways that are pleasing to you. Allow me to be your guide, but then, most of all, enjoy beading to your own drummer.

Once upon a time

We all have our bead stories; mine is simply that I want to share what I have loved for as long as I can remember. Beads are my passion. I want to teach and inspire. My journey has been an evolution; one stitch or variation has led to another. Just when I think I have invented a new stitch, I see it somewhere else. I began with peyote and from there I started experimenting with other stitches. I love to see where one stitch will take me, how simply playing with the beads can take me to a new level, a new idea. If anything here looks like something you have made or tried, please know that this is simply the hand of creative fate and coincidence. Many minds think alike, and while we are all looking for that next great stitch, we will uncover many more along the way, many that others have already figured out. I am constantly thinking about what I can do next, thinking "What would happen if…?"

Thank you for allowing me to share my work with you. Now, if you are ready to begin, grab a needle, a comfortable length of beading thread, and some beads. Oh, and grab a piece of chocolate. You may need it.

Beth

BASICS AND SUPPLIES

Bead stitching, also known as off-loom beadweaving, is the art of creating beaded fabric using only a needle, thread, and assorted beads. The beads most often used to create these stitched fabrics are called seed beads. Seed beads can be found in bead stores, some craft stores, and on the Internet. There seems to be an endless supply as this art becomes more and more popular. Different bead shapes and sizes will create different stitch variations depending on bead placement and order. The main theme throughout this book is: "Don't be afraid to experiment!"

Seed beads

When I was a young girl, my grandmother (of blessed memory) and my mother, both avid beaders, made hundreds of beautiful beaded flowers. They also embellished some of their clothing with bead embroidery. I remember looking at their stash of beads wishing they were mine, imagining what I could do with them. When I was given some of their beads to play with, I was hooked. Unfortunately, seed beads back then were available in a very limited number of colors and sizes. Today, seed beads can be found in so many colors, sizes, shapes, and finishes that it is sometimes hard to know what to buy or where to begin. If you are as addicted as I am, you probably have small amounts of everything! If you are just beginning, you'll have your own bead stash in a very short time.

Seed beads are sized by number, and range from 2° (6mm) to 24° (smaller than 1mm). The higher the number associated with the bead, the smaller the bead. You will hear bead sizes described as a number, such as "elevens," or see them as a number with a symbol, such as 11/0 or 11° (pronounced "eleven aught"). The most common seed bead size is 11°, but most suppliers carry sizes ranging from 6° (also called E beads) to 15°. 14°s and 15°s are interchangeable. Seed beads smaller than 15° are difficult to work with as their holes are tiny. They're also rather scarce – most of these minute sizes are no longer manufactured. Seed beads larger than 6° are not something that I use in my work.

The most common and highest quality seed beads today are manufactured in Japan or the Czech Republic. These seed beads are the most uniform and predictable in size, shape, and hole size, plus they're available in an amazing range of colors.

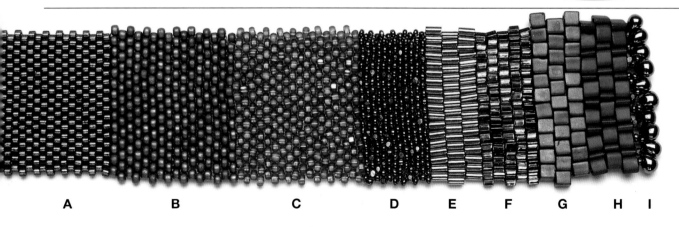

A   B   C   D   E   F   G   H   I

Japanese cylinder beads

Japanese cylinder beads (A) are tubular in shape, with thin walls and large holes that allow many thread passes. They are very consistent in size and can be found in hundreds of colors and finishes. They are most frequently sold as size 11°, but can be found as 8°s (sometimes called 3.3s) and 10°s, too. Because cylinder beads are so consistent in size and shape, they don't require much culling (culling is the act of removing inferior or badly sized beads before you begin a project). Cylinder bead brands include Miyuki Delicas, Toho Treasures, and Toho Aikos. Other brands also are available.

Cylinder beads create a more angular look than you would get when working with rounder seed beads. While cylinder beads are beautiful and easy to use, they don't add much texture to a piece of beadwoven fabric. Cylinder beads are, however, the perfect choice for my "stained glass" designs (p. 19).

Japanese seed beads

Japanese seed beads (B) are rounder than cylinder beads, which makes them a good choice when you want to add texture and visual interest to your piece. They come in a range of sizes, but 8°s, 11°s, and 15°s are the easiest to find. While they aren't as precisely shaped as cylinder beads, Japanese seed beads are very consistent in shape and size, so they don't require much culling. Like cylinder beads, they come in a wide range of colors and finishes.

Czech seed beads

Czech seed beads (C) are rounder than Japanese seed beads. They are less consistent in size and shape and require more culling. And again, because they are rounder and differ a little in shape and size, they too add a bit more texture and visual interest to a piece of beaded fabric.

Charlottes

Charlottes (D), also known as one-cut or true cuts, have a cut (facet) on one side which gives the bead a wonderful sparkle. While 13° is the traditional and probably most common size of Charlottes, you can also find Charlottes in sizes 6°, 8°, 11°, and 15°. Charlottes can have tiny or irregular holes, so you often need to use a smaller needle when working with them.

Bugle beads

Bugle beads (E) are long, tube-shaped beads that range in size from about 1/8 in. to more than 1½ in. Like seed beads, bugle beads are manufactured in Japan and the Czech Republic, but each country uses a different numbering system to size the beads. It can be confusing, but in general, the larger the number, the longer the beads. Some bugle beads are twisted, which can add texture to your woven pieces. Bugle beads are notorious for having sharp edges that can cut through some beading threads, so you may want to cull out the beads with broken or sharp ends. Some beaders file their bugle beads.

Other seed bead shapes

Seed beads also come in a variety of shapes such as hexagons (F), cubes (G), triangles (H), and teardrops (I). All of the shapes can be found in several sizes.

Seed bead colors and finishes

As if all of these shapes and sizes were not fun enough, seed beads are available in a wide variety of colors and surface finishes. Some of these finishes are listed below:

- **Aurora Borealis** or **AB** (1) is a rainbow effect created by applying the finish to hot glass. This rainbow effect is often called "iris" when it's applied to metallic beads.
- **Ceylon** (2) is a pearl-like finish (sometimes known as pearlized).
- **Dyed** (3) finishes can be found on Japanese seed beads. This finish will wear off if you don't seal the beads before using them. I try to stay away from dyed beads.
- **Luster** (4, 9) is a very shiny finish.
- **Metallic** (5) finish gives the beads a look resembling metal. While most metallic finishes are stable, some, like galvanized finishes, may wear off over time.
- **Matte** (1) beads are usually tumbled or frosted to give them a flat (non-shiny) appearance.
- **Opaque** (1, 5, 6) beads are solid-colored beads; you cannot see through them.
- **Lined** (4, 7, 9) beads are usually transparent or translucent and have a metallic or opaque coating on the hole.
- **Satin** (8) finish has a striated, satiny look.
- **Transparent** (7, 9) beads are fairly clear – you can see through them. The color of thread you are using could change the appearance of the bead.
- **Translucent** (2, 8) beads allow light to pass through them.

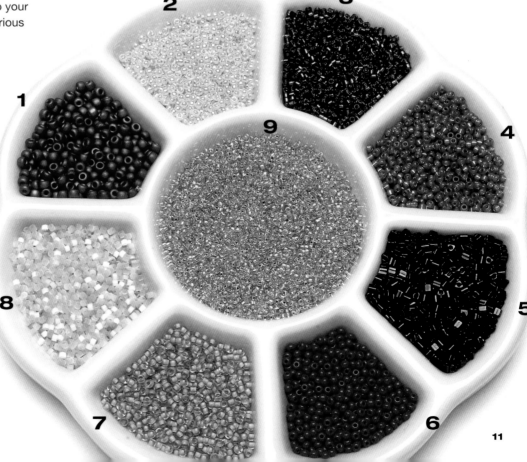

Beading thread

The subject of beading thread can get you into a discussion that will never end. Long or short? Waxed or unwaxed? Nymo, Silamide, C-Lon, SoNo, or Fireline? We all have our favorite thread and way to use it. You may need to experiment with all of them to find yours.

Silamide thread has been used in the tailoring industry for years. It is a pre-waxed, two-ply twisted thread that resists fraying. It has gained popularity in the beading world in the past few years. Silamide is strong and is available in a variety of colors, which is why it's my current favorite.

A wide variety of single-ply nylon threads are available. Nymo is a very popular type of nylon monofilament beading thread. It is flat, untwisted, and comes in a variety of colors. The thickness of the thread is labeled with letters A–F, plus O, OO, and OOO. In general, the closer to the beginning of the alphabet, the thinner the thread, except the Os, which are thinner than A (OOO being the thinnest). The most popular sizes are D and B. Nymo will fray if you have to take out mistakes often or if you use a very long thread. Nymo also twists while you work with it.

C-Lon, developed by Caravan Beads, was born out of the desire for a product somewhere between Nymo and Silamide. C-Lon is offered in two sizes: D (similar in size to Nymo D) and AA (similar in size to Silamide). C-Lon is available in a variety of permanently dyed colors and is resistant to fraying.

SoNo was designed by Japanese master beader Sonoko Nozue to be a cross between Nymo and Silamide. Since this popular thread was introduced to North America, Ms. Nozue has developed an improved version of the thread, called K.O. K.O. has a rounder profile and comes pre-waxed, making it even more fray-resistant than SoNo. Toho, a competing company, has put out its own beading thread with these characteristics, One-G.

Fireline is a strong, durable fishing line made of polyethylene that is a new favorite among beaders. It doesn't stretch, and it's particularly good for stitching with sharp-edged beads, since it is strong. The smoke color is almost invisible in most beading projects, while the new crystal Fireline can be used with transparent beads (but may look white). Fireline can be found in many bead stores as well as large sporting goods or fishing stores. Fireline is available in 4 lb., 6 lb., 8 lb., and higher strengths, but 6 lb. and 8 lb. are most appropriate for beadwork. Some Fireline has a thin, dark coating that has a tendency to rub off on your fingers and lighter color beads. Try using a cloth to rub off as much as possible to prevent this from happening. There are several other brands of polyethylene thread available, most notably Power Pro and Dandyline, which are made of Spectra Fiber and are also sturdy and useful for some beading applications. (I would not recommend stitching with monofilament fishing lines, as they can become brittle over time and break.)

Thread wax and conditioners

I must confess that I do not use a thread wax or conditioner in my beadwork (because I use Fireline and Silamide), but I know there are many beaders who can't and won't work without it (these beaders usually use Nymo, SoNo, or C-Lon). I did my homework, however, and found that while there are a few products that are used as thread conditioners, only one was created by a beader specifically for the purpose of making beading easier.

Thread Heaven, created by Roni Hennen, is a thread conditioner and protectant that both reduces thread tangling, knotting, and fraying, while at the same time protects the

integrity of the thread. This patented product was created to make thread more manageable and to extend the life of your beadwork. It adds a static charge to the thread, so it repels itself and is less likely to tangle. For more information visit her Web site at threadheaven.com.

The most traditional product for conditioning thread is beeswax, which usually comes in a bar or round cake. Beeswax adds a fullness to the thread that adds tension and helps the beads sit more stiffly when stitched – qualities some beaders find necessary when working certain stitches.

According to Roni Hennen, "Using Thread Heaven and wax together can often produce a best-of-both-worlds situation. For example, coating the thread with Thread Heaven, then with wax, will protect it from the acidity and the additional drag of the wax, while the topcoat of wax will impart the additional tension many beaders feel is necessary to work certain types of stitches."

Beading needles

I use English beading needles exclusively in my work. There are two kinds: sharp and beading. Sharps are shorter and stiffer than beading needles. Personal preference and comfort will dictate the type of needle you should use. The #12 beading needle is perfect for most off-loom beadwork. If you have trouble threading this needle you may want to try the #11 or #10, but keep in mind that the smaller the needle number, the thicker the needle. Some beadwork (like the spiral stitch) requires many passes of thread through each bead, so a thinner needle will work better. I have not had any problems using a #12 needle with size 15º seed beads.

Other beading needles available are twisted wire needles, Big Eye needles, and Japanese beading needles. Of these, Japanese beading needles are the most appropriate for stitching projects.

Bead dishes and mats

Invest in a few porcelain multi-compartment beading dishes. They're great for sorting beads by size and color. Stay away from the plastic look-alikes as they will become very static and your beads will take on a life of their own.

Bead mats made of a foam-like material work well on a flat surface. I recommend using a mat-lined tray with sides when beading on your lap or in the car (as a passenger, please).

Scissors and wire cutters

Regular scissors will cut through all of the beading threads with the exception of Fireline. For this, I use basic wire cutters dedicated to cutting Fireline.

Lighting

There was a time when I could bead in the dark. Then time started catching up with me (and my eyes). While a number of beaders swear by the Ott-lite, I bead with a desk lamp over my shoulder. As long as there is light, I can bead. You will need to figure out what works best for you.

Magnifiers

My eye doctor warned me that my near vision would get blurry as I got older, and he was right. One day I could see the tiny beads up close and the next day I was wearing 2.5 magnifying glasses. Magnifying glasses can be purchased in drug stores as well as department stores. Some beaders use magnifying lamps, which allow for extra light as well as extra magnification. Again, you will have to figure out what works best for you.

TERMS I USE THROUGHOUT THE BOOK

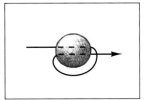

Stop bead: This bead is attached to the end of the beading thread (leaving a tail for finishing) to keep the first beads strung from falling off the end. It's especially useful for beginners. String the stop bead, then go through it again in the same direction. Alternatively, you could tie an overhand knot around the bead. The stop bead is removed before you work in the tail and finish the piece.

Length of beading thread: Try to use the longest piece of beading thread that you are comfortable with. Some projects use a lot of thread (the spiral stitch, for example), while other stitches don't require as much.

Thread tail: Leave at least 10–12 in. of thread as a tail at the beginning and end of all projects. You will need this thread to attach your closures and clasps.

Working thread: This is the side of the thread to which your needle is attached.

Knots: Some beaders use a wide range of knots, and know the appropriate use for all of them. The simple overhand knot (bring one end under another and pull) and a square knot (go under and pull again) should be enough to get you started.

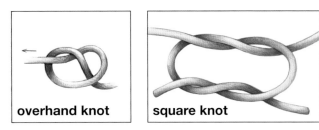

Bead soup: I don't know the origin of this term, but it's used to describe a collection of beads left over from other projects. Using bead soup may introduce some interesting color combinations. Some people create their own bead soup to get just the right color mix.

Tension: One of the most important aspects of bead stitching is keeping your tension tight and consistent. It may take some practice to get a feel for what the right tension should be. Everyone holds their beadwork differently. With practice and patience, you will find what works well for you.

Picot surface embellishment: Adding surface embellishment is a fun and easy way to add texture to an otherwise regular surface. I especially like to add this type of texture to bead-stitched ropes and tubes, for added dimension. Instructions for how to add picot surface embellishments are explained in Chapter 1, p. 29. Look for references to this technique throughout the book.

Finish as desired: There's no one right way to finish a piece of beaded jewelry. You can use metal clasps, buttons, large glass or pearl beads, or my favorite, the beaded loop and toggle. This last technique creates a seamless finish that flows right out of the beadwork. There is a lot of room for creativity in closures – check out "Bead Play" in Chapter 1, p. 30, for more on stitching your own toggle clasp.

To add any closure, use a long tail or secure a new thread in the beadwork (see "Changing threads," below), and exit where you want to add the clasp. Depending on the type of clasp you use, you might want to pick up a few beads to create a loop or add some space between the clasp and the beadwork. Otherwise, pick up the clasp, and weave back into the beadwork. Clasps suffer a lot of stress and wear and tear, so be sure to weave through the beadwork and reinforce the join several times.

Changing threads: It's time to start a new thread when you have about 6 in. of the working thread left. Thread a new needle with the new thread. Start a few rows back, leave a tail, and weave this new thread through the beadwork. Be careful that your thread doesn't go through the circles and empty spaces that your beadwork had created. You don't want this new thread to be visible. You may want to tie a few knots around the existing thread as you weave. Come out where the existing thread exits, and resume beading with the new thread. After a few rows, weave in the tails, and trim the thread. When you finish a project, you'll weave the starting and ending tails into the beadwork the same way.

WHAT I WON'T TELL YOU...

What colors to use: If I list colors in the materials list or directions, they are simply the colors that I used, and I listed them to add clarity to the instructions. Please choose colors that are pleasing to you. Part of the fun of beading is the creative color play. A bead-stitched piece of art will take on a different life when worked in different colors.

Exactly how many beads you will need: I wish I knew exactly how many beads are used in any one project, but the truth is that you need to buy an entire tube of beads or strand of pearls no matter what. So use what you need and then put away the rest for another project. The materials list at the beginning of each project will tell you what you need but not necessarily how much or how many.

A finished length: We all like (and need) different lengths for our jewelry. Bracelet lengths usually range from 6–8 in., while necklaces can be 16 in. (choker length), 18 in. (sitting just below the collarbone), 20 in., 24 in., 30 in., and longer. Try your piece on from time to time to check the length. The important thing to remember is that adding a clasp will add length to your piece.

Peyote Stitch

chapter 1

Peyote stitch, also known as gourd stitch, is one of my favorite stitches, and the basis for many of my projects and variations. While not a difficult stitch, it can be tricky to learn as you try to figure out just how to hold your work and how to get the right tension. The first time I attempted this stitch I threw it across the room, but I picked it up, kept at it, and now love it. If you get frustrated, just remember that with a little practice you too will get it and then wonderful things will happen!

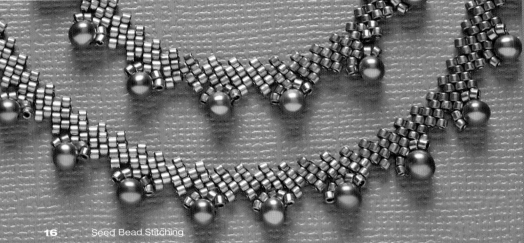

The first thing you need to know about peyote is what it looks like.

Imagine a brick wall ....

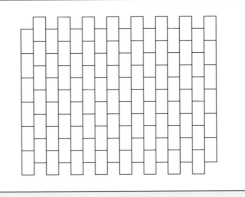

Now turn it on its side: This is what a small piece of finished "even-count" peyote fabric will look like. (Even-count refers to the number of vertical columns.) There are some basic characteristics that are unique to this stitch.

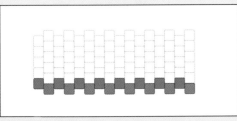

Look closely at the picture, and you will see that there are no perfectly straight horizontal lines, only the illusion of a line.

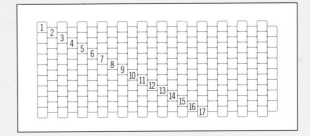

There are, however, straight vertical lines as well as stepped diagonal lines.

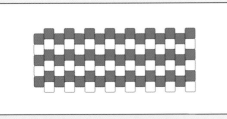

Flat peyote is often worked horizontally (back and forth) with rows added vertically. The rows nestle together, so when you stitch a new row, you leave spaces between the beads. You will fill the spaces as you stitch the next row, but then you'll create a new set of spaces to fill.

In the diagram, the purple beads are Row 1 and the green beads are Row 2. Notice that the Row 1 beads are sticking out: I'll call these "protruding" beads. The row 2 beads are set back, so I'll call them "recessed" beads.

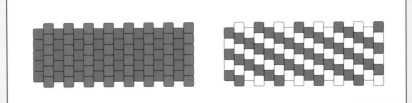

An important thing to know about peyote is that you count your rows on the diagonal.

This could make your eyes cross as you lose count and have to start again.

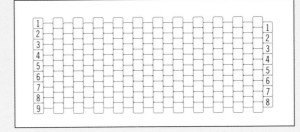

An easier way to count the rows of even-count peyote is to count the number of beads on each flat side and add them.
9 + 8 = 17!

BASIC PEYOTE

Even-count flat peyote is the easiest and most basic peyote variation. Even-count peyote will have an even number of vertical columns. New rows start the same way on both sides, so the process is consistent and symmetrical. (Odd-count peyote has one type of turn on one side and a more complicated turn on the other side. The turns for odd-count can be tricky, so when I'm creating a peyote piece that needs a single center bead column, I use brick stitch – see "Bead Play," Chapter 2, p. 38, to learn this trick.) Once you understand how basic peyote works, it's easy to learn the other variations.

PROJECT

Black-and-White Band

A simple strap bracelet using two contrasting colors of Japanese cylinder beads is a great beginning project. You will learn how to create various stripes and geometric patterns within your fabric as you're learning the basics of peyote stitch.

MATERIALS:
- matte black Japanese cylinder beads
- matte white Japanese cylinder beads
- beading thread
- size 10 or 12 beading needle

Beginning beaders may want to tie a stop bead onto the beading thread to keep the beads from coming off (see p. 14).

1. Beginning with a black bead, string ten beads of alternating colors onto your beading thread. These ten beads will make up the first two rows.

2. Pick up a white bead (#11). Turn around and go back into bead #9 (a black bead) skipping over beads #11 and 10 (**photo a**). You will be working back toward the tail.

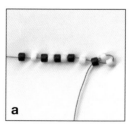
a

3. Pick up a white bead (#12) and pass your needle through the next black bead, #7 (**photo b**).

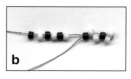
b

4. Pick up bead #13 and pass your needle through bead #5.

5. Pick up bead #14 and go through bead #3. Pick up bead #15 and go through bead #1. You have now completed your first three rows.

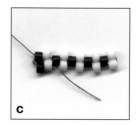
c

6. Begin the next row by picking up a black bead, #16, and going into the nearest protruding white bead, #15 (**photo c**).

7. Continue stitching the row, picking up black beads (#17, 18, 19, and 20) one at a time and going through the protruding white beads (#14, 13, 12, and 11, respectively), as before.

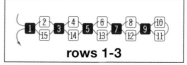
rows 1-3

8. Stitch the next row adding white beads, once again going through the protruding black beads. Notice that you are creating vertical stripes.

9. Continue working each row, alternating black and white beads, until you have a total of 15 rows (**photo d**). Remember to count your rows on the diagonal or count the flat sides and add them up.

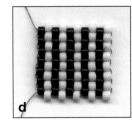
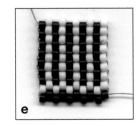

d

10. You are now ready to start the next segment of the bracelet, the horizontal "illusion" striping. This is created by stitching at least two rows of the same color. Stitch the first row with white beads, going through the white beads from the previous row.

11. Stitch two rows of black beads (**photo e**).

e

12. Stitch two white rows, two black rows, two white rows, two black rows, and two white rows (**photo f**).

Continue following the pattern below to create more fun geometric segments. You will begin on row #29, alternating black and white beads on each stitch, as shown. (Turn the bracelet pattern on its side and count down 14 rows on the left side of the pattern to quickly see where you are). This bracelet is 7¾ in. long. To make it longer, try repeating a segment. To make it shorter, try eliminating a segment.

I finished this bracelet with a tube clasp, but feel free to experiment with your own ideas. For information on attaching a clasp, see p. 14 and p. 30.

f

top

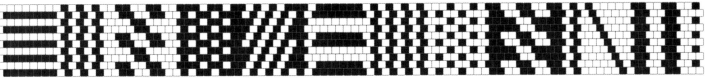

bracelet pattern

More geometric patterns

Now that you know how to work peyote stitch and read a peyote chart, you can experiment with the wide variety of patterns available, and even make your own. Here are a few more examples of ways to use geometric patterns. You can create pins, pendants, and more bracelets.

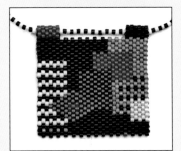

This pendant was very easy to create – it's a simple rectangle with a fun color pattern. Notice how the black background helps the colors stand out.

A pendant featuring triangular points and dangles makes a strong statement. It's easy to make triangular points on a peyote piece. Instead of turning and adding a bead, sew under the thread bridge between the bead you exited and the previous row, come back through the bead you just exited, and continue through the last bead added. The playful effect here is enhanced by the asymmetrical necklace; the bold 6°s on one side are balanced by two strands of 11°s on the other side.

Here, I stitched tabs above the pendant. I attached the ends of the tabs to the back of the pendant, forming loops (also known as bails) that I used to hang the pendant on my necklace.

DIAGONAL PEYOTE

By working an alternating pattern of increases and decreases, you can make peyote stitch form diagonal lines. There are a variety of ways to do this, but my favorite way is to increase or decrease an even number of columns in each row. Because it may be difficult to see how this stitch works at first, make sure you have a good understanding of even-count peyote and how to work it. The illustration and photos show each increase and decrease in a different color for clarity.

First, work a peyote patch that is eight beads wide and eight rows long (four beads on each flat side). This patch is not part of the diagonal peyote pattern, but it gives you a good foundation to work from as you're learning the new stitch.

There are eight vertical columns in this sample. You will make a simple two-column increase that will increase the number of vertical columns from eight to ten.

Having just added the last bead in the row, and with your needle coming out of the last bead of the column, pick up three beads. Turn around and go back through the first of the three beads.

Continue across the row, adding the next three beads. Stop with your needle coming out of the second-to-last protruding bead, instead of completing the row. This is where you will do a decrease. You added two columns on the right side of this sample; you'll now eliminate two columns on the left side. Pick up a new bead, turn, and go through the next protruding bead.

Finish this row, adding three beads. With your needle coming out of the end bead, pick up three beads to make another two-column increase. Turn around and go back through the first of the three beads. Pull tight to your beadwork.

Stitch the next three beads in the row. Do another two-column decrease by turning at the second-to-last protruding bead. Pick up the next bead and go through the next protruding bead.

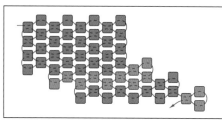

Finish this row by stitching the next three beads, and do the next two-column increase. The beadwork will continue to form a diagonal band as you work.

PROJECT
Simple Strap Bracelet

Now that you see how diagonal peyote works, you can use it in a variety of ways. Here's a simple strap bracelet using Japanese cylinder beads to get you started. Don't be afraid to experiment as you get comfortable with this stitch.

MATERIALS:
- Japanese cylinder beads
- beading thread
- size 10 or 12 beading needle

1. Pick up six Japanese cylinder beads.

2. Pick up bead #7, skip bead #6, and pass your needle through bead #5.

3. Work peyote to the end, adding two beads, #8 and #9 (**photo a**).

4. Turn and work peyote to the end again, adding three beads (#10, 11, and 12).

5. Make the first increase by picking up three beads (#13, 14, and 15). Turn and go back into the first bead you just picked up (#13). Pull tight to beadwork (**photo b**).

6. Continue stitching the row, adding the next two beads (#16 and 17). Remember, this is where you will do a decrease, so you will not work any further than this. (Your thread should be coming out of bead #11.)

7. Turn. Pick up bead #18, turn, and go through bead #17 (**photo c**).

8. Repeat steps 3–7 until you reach your desired length. (My bracelet is 6½ in. long.)
   Finish this bracelet with a metal clasp or make your own toggle clasp (see "Bead Play," p. 30, for more on making your own clasp).

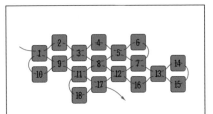

steps 1-7

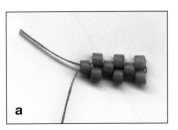

a

b

c

Diagonal peyote variations

Diagonal peyote is typically worked with an alternating increase and decrease in every row, as demonstrated by the bracelet on p. 21. You can create a number of interesting variations by varying the bead counts and using beads of different colors, shapes, and sizes.

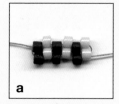

a

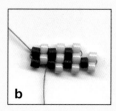

b

Color striping

It's easy to create a striped pattern in diagonal peyote. Two contrasting colors of Japanese cylinder beads are perfect for this variation.

Pick up six beads, alternating colors. We'll call them color A and color B. Work the third row using color A beads. Work the fourth row using color B beads (**photo a**). If you made the geometric black and white bracelet at the beginning of the chapter, this should seem familiar to you!

To do the two-column increase, pick up one color B and two color A beads. Skip the color A beads and sew back through the color B bead. Pull the increase tight to the beadwork. Stitch two more color A beads and turn to make the decrease (**photo b**). Work the three stitches back to the other end using color B beads. You'll always pick up an A before going through a B, and pick up a B before going through an A, just like in striped flat peyote.

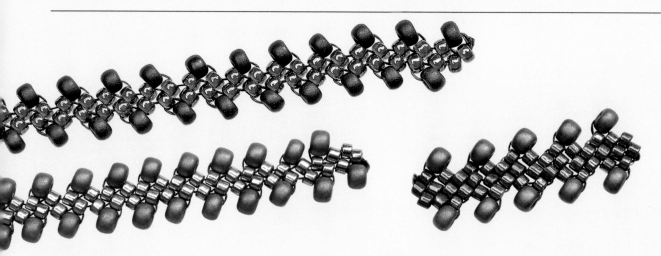

Mixed beads

You can mix bead sizes to create a different look. Try using 8ºs with cylinder beads or 11ºs. To make these easy chains, pick up three cylinder beads (or 11ºs), an 8º, and a cylinder. Skip the last cylinder and 8º, and go back through the next cylinder. Pick up one more cylinder to finish the row (**photo a**).

Pick up an 8º to make the turn, and go through the last cylinder added. Pick up a cylinder and finish the row (**photo b**).

Stitch the piece as though it were normal diagonal peyote, increasing and decreasing every other row (**photo c**). When you make a two-column increase, pick up a cylinder, an 8º, and a cylinder for the three beads. When you turn to make a decrease, pick up an 8º instead of a cylinder. It's that easy.

a

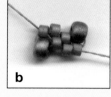

b

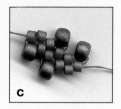

c

Wide-Row Earrings

These playful earrings space out the increases and decreases to create a pattern of stepped rectangles.

1. Pick up eight cylinder beads to form your first two rows. Turn, pick up a cylinder, skip a cylinder, and go through the next cylinder. Continue stitching in flat, even-count peyote until you have ten rows (or eight rows, if you'd like a more symmetrical diagonal).

2. At the end of the eighth row, make a four-column increase: Pick up five cylinder beads, skip the last two beads, and go back through the third bead. Pick up a cylinder, and go through the first bead of the increase (**photo a**).

3. Make two more peyote stitches across the row, then turn to make the decrease. Pick up a cylinder, and go through the next protruding bead. Stitch to the end of the row, and continue stitching until you have a second segment of eight rows (**photo b**).

4. Repeat steps 2 and 3 until your earring is as long as you like.

5. To add a pearl dangle to the bottom, come out the bottom protruding bead of the last segment. Pick up a cylinder, a pearl, and a cylinder. Go back through the pearl, pick up a cylinder, and weave back into the beadwork through the bead you exited. Weave in the tail and trim.

6. Thread a needle on the starting tail and pick up five cylinder beads. Go through the adjacent cylinder in the next row and the same bead you exited in the same direction to make a loop. Go through the cylinders again, and weave the tail into the beadwork. Attach this loop to the loop of an earring finding.

7. Make a second earring, and attach the earring finding so it hangs as a mirror image of the first.

MATERIALS:
- Japanese cylinder beads
- 2 freshwater pearls
- pair of earring findings
- beading thread
- size 10 or 12 beading needle

a

b

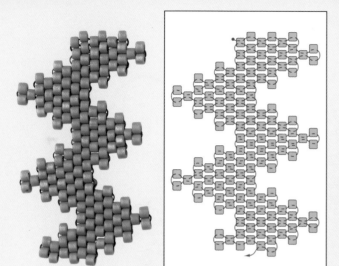

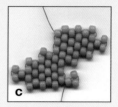 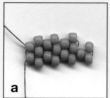 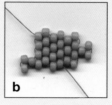

Zigzags

Here, diagonal peyote is used, but after you stitch a few rows you switch the increases and decreases, changing the direction of the fabric. Start by picking up six beads. Work peyote stitch for four rows, and then do a two-column increase. For row 5, work all the way to the end instead of doing a decrease (**photo a**). Turn, and work three stitches, a decrease. Turn, work three stitches to the end of the row, and then make a two-column increase. Work the next two stitches, then turn, making a decrease (**photo b**). Work the three stitches to the end of the row, and make a two-column increase (**photo c**). Work two stitches, making a decrease at the end of the row. For row 11, work three stitches to the end of the row, and make a two-column increase. Keep working back and forth like this, repeating rows 5–11, and you'll soon have a nice zigzag pattern.

Dangles

I love the look of necklaces strung with suspended pearls, stones, or glass beads. I was inspired to make my first woven neckpiece after seeing a gorgeous (and very expensive) necklace by artist Susan Hoge. I have no idea what her technique is, so I figured out something that would work for me. In honor of her, I titled my first necklace, "Thank You, Susan." Coming up with a technique was relatively easy. The question for me was, "How can I make this work with just one thread path?" After a few attempts I figured it out. Actually, I figured it out twice – the type of stone, glass bead, or pearl you are adding will make a difference in the way you attach it to the woven neck strap. I am constantly amazed at how one technique can create such different looks depending on the beads used.

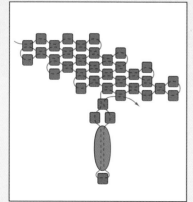

Top-to-bottom dangles

Start by stitching diagonal peyote, alternating a two-column increase on one side with a two-column decrease on the other. When you get to where you want to place the first dangle, exit the beadwork as though you were turning to make a decrease.

Pick up two seed beads, one drop bead, and one seed bead. Skip the last seed bead, and go back up though the drop bead. Pick up a bead, skip the bead sitting right on top of the drop bead, and go back through the next seed bead and the next protruding bead. Continue working diagonal peyote as usual, but add drop beads as often as you would like.

Top-drilled dangles

Modifying the top-to-bottom dangle stitch to work with top-drilled beads is easy. (See the step-by-step project on the next page to find out how easy it is!) Depending on how you space your dangles, you can use all types of beads. Try small teardrop pearls spaced close together, or dramatic stones spaced farther apart.

PROJECT

Freshwater Pearl Necklace

You can make this beautiful, sophisticated necklace in just a few hours. It's a basic variation of diagonal peyote stitch, with a modification to attach top-drilled beads.

MATERIALS:
- Japanese cylinder beads
- top-drilled freshwater pearls
- beading thread
- size 10 or 12 beading needle

1. Pick up six cylinder beads, turn, and begin stitching in diagonal peyote (as in the bracelet on p. 21). After you've stitched the fourth row, pick up three beads (#13, 14, and 15) and do the first increase. Continue in diagonal peyote, increasing and decreasing on every row until you have eight rows of diagonal peyote. Exit the beadwork as though you were turning to make a decrease (coming out of bead #27).

2. Pick up three seed beads, one top-drilled pearl, and two seed beads (**photo a**). Depending on where the hole is in your pearl, you may need to add or subtract one seed bead from each side of the pearl.

3. Form a circle with the beads by going back through bead #34 in the same direction as before.

4. Continue through bead #33 to secure.

5. Finish the row, working two more stitches (**photo b**).

6. Do an increase and continue working diagonal peyote, adding the pearls as often as you would like, until you reach your desired length.

7. Finish with a closure of your choice. (I stitched a peyote toggle closure and a peyote loop for my necklace).

a

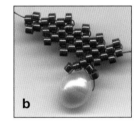

b

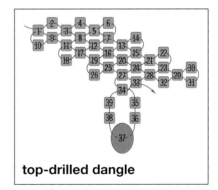

top-drilled dangle

Lightning bolts

My first lightning bracelet began as a "mistake." While beginning a diagonal peyote necklace, I did my first increase at the end of row 3 instead of row 4 (step 1 of the previous project). Here is a picture of what I was supposed to do (**photo a**). Notice which beads the tails are coming out of.

Here is a picture of what I actually did (**photo b**). I noticed that this piece took on a curvy "S" shape when I pulled at the two tails in the second example. I really liked the way this looked and, after a bit of experimentation, "Pearled Lightning" was born.

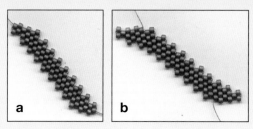

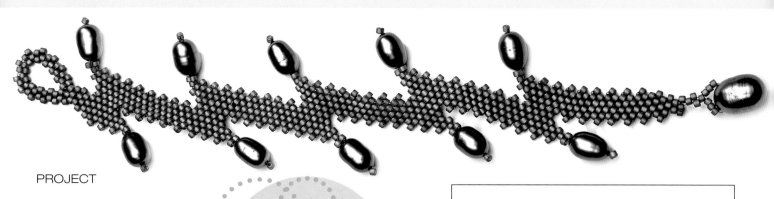

PROJECT

Pearled Lightning

The first pearled lightning bracelet consisted of six pieces that I sewed together. It took me about two weeks to figure out how to make this bracelet in one thread path. Now this bracelet always turns heads.

MATERIALS:
- Japanese cylinder beads
- freshwater pearls
- large top-drilled freshwater pearl for the closure
- beading thread
- size 10 or 12 beading needle

You'll use two different methods for adding the pearls to the "lightning bolts." One pearl addition will be called "pearl addition A," and the other will be called "pearl addition B."

1. Pick up 12 Japanese cylinder beads, one large top-drilled freshwater pearl, and three cylinders. Skip the last three cylinders, the pearl, and the three previous cylinders, and go back through the next cylinder. Peyote stitch to the end of the row and flip your work over (**photo a**).

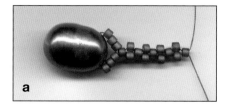

2. Pick up three cylinders (#21, 22, and 23), and go back through #21, a two-column increase. Stitch three cylinders (#24, 25, and 26), then stop. You'll now make a decrease (**photo b**).

3. Turn, pick up a cylinder (#27), and go through the next protruding cylinder (#26). Stitch to the end of the row, adding three cylinders, #28, 29, and 30.

4. Make a two-column increase, as in step 2. Continue in diagonal peyote until you have completed 26 vertical columns. Start counting from the first two-bead column from the large pearl.

5. Pearl addition A: Pick up two cylinders (#111 and 112 in the illustration), one pearl (#113), and a cylinder (#114). Skip the last cylinder added, go back through the pearl, pick up a cylinder (#115) and go through the second bead from the pearl, #111 (**photo c**).

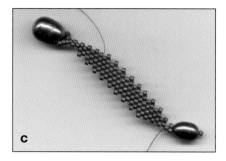

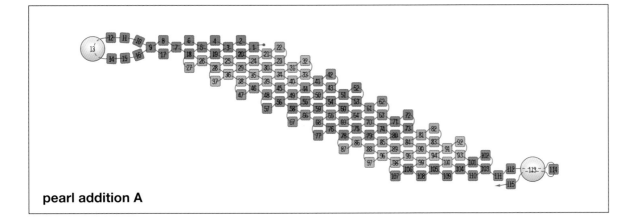

pearl addition A

6. Continue working peyote all the way to the end of the row, adding four cylinders (#116, 117, 118, and 119). Turn and work peyote for three stitches (#120, 121, and 122).

7. Pearl addition B: Your needle should be coming out of the end bead of the four-bead column closest to the pearl just added (#117). Without picking up any beads, weave back through the beadwork to exit the first bead added in the last row, bead #120 in the illustration (**photo d**).

8. Pick up five cylinders (#123, 124, 125, 126, and 127), a pearl (#128), and a cylinder (#129). Turn, and go back through the pearl. Pick up a cylinder (#130), skip a cylinder, and go through the next cylinder, #126 (**photo e**).

9. Work peyote for four stitches, then turn and work back for four stitches. Turn again, and work four more stitches (**photo f**).

10. Pick up three beads (#143, 144, and 145) for a two-column increase. Then, continue with peyote for three stitches, and turn to continue stitching diagonal peyote until you have 26 vertical columns counting from the pearl addition B.

11. Repeat steps 5–10 to continue the bracelet, alternating pearl addition A and pearl addition B, until your bracelet almost fits around your wrist.

12. Pick up enough beads to create a circle that will barely fit around the large pearl (**photo g**). You can peyote stitch the circle of beads to make it more stable (see p. 30). This makes the clasp of the bracelet. Weave in the tails and trim the thread.

d

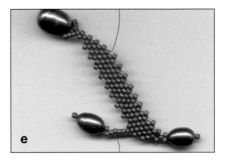

e

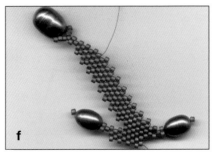

f

g

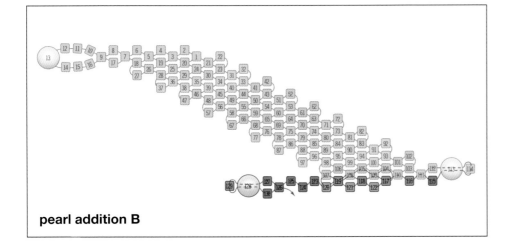

pearl addition B

TUBULAR PEYOTE

This rope is a fun variation of the peyote stitch. You will begin with three beads and work in the round. Each row will have a simple "step-up" – an easy step that will become clear as you begin the instructions. You can create variations using beads of different sizes and colors. I use a surface embellishment technique that adds great texture to my pieces.

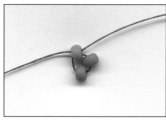

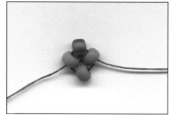

To show you how to stitch tubular peyote, I'll use two colors, alternating colors on each row. Alternating the colors this way makes stripes, just like in the bracelet at the start of the chapter.

First, pick up three beads in color A. Create a circle by going through the first bead again in the same direction. You should have thread coming out of both sides of the bead.

With your thread coming out of bead #1, pick up a color B bead. Go through bead #2.

Pick up a color B bead and go through bead #3. Then, pick up another color B and go through bead #1.

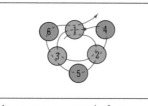

You are now ready for the "step-up" in order to begin the next row. With your thread coming out of bead #1, pass your needle through bead #4. That's it – you've stepped up.

Pick up an A bead and go through the next B bead, bead #5. Repeat a round using As, and then step up through the first bead of the new round to get in position to stitch the next round of Bs. Pull the third round of beads up to make a tube shape. Continue until your tube is the desired length.

Love, Cheyenne – a bracelet
After showing my then-10-year-old daughter, Cheyenne, how to make a tubular peyote rope, she took it upon herself to create this colorful, fun bracelet. I have to admit that I was pretty impressed by her sense of color and design. Using bright blocks of color, you can stitch one of your own.

Here's the pattern: 14 rows of color A, two rows of color B, 14 rows of color A. Then repeat, but use color B beads for the long section and color C beads for the two rows in the middle. Continue following the pattern, using a new color for each repetition.

Tubular peyote variations

You can achieve many interesting results by varying the bead counts and using beads of different shapes and sizes in tubular peyote. *Experiment* as you learn more about peyote stitch – you'll be surprised by the variations you discover on your own.

Mixed sizes

It's easy to make a textured rope by changing the bead sizes every few rows. You can make the changes part of a pattern, using the same beads for several rows, as in the necklace below, or change bead sizes and shapes drastically every few rows. If the difference between bead sizes is extreme, you may need to pick up two beads for each stitch as you stitch the smaller beads.

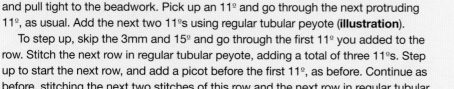

Spirals

You can create a fun effect by adding 8º's to your 11º tube. After you step up to begin a new row, pick up an 8º as the first bead of the new row (**illustration**). Complete the rest of the row with 11ºs in tubular peyote, as usual. When you step up through the 8º to start the next row, pick up another 8º as the first bead, and stitch this row like the last. As you continue around the tube, adding an 8º after every step-up, the 8ºs will spiral around the tube (**photo a**).

You can create spirals of color, too. Simply change the color of the last bead of the row. Here, an 8º is added after the step-up, then a blue 11º, and then a green 11º. After the step-up, the pattern is repeated (**photo b**).

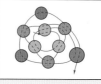

Embellishments

The possibilities for surface embellishment are nearly endless. Two of my favorites are picots and points.

Picots

After finishing a stitch, pick up three 11ºs or 15ºs and pass your needle back into the bead you are coming out of to create a circle (**photo a**). This creates a small loop surface embellishment called a picot. If you add this loop to the step-up bead at the beginning of each row, the picots will spiral around the tube (**photo b**).

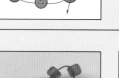

Points

To create three rows of embellishments down the sides of the tube, as in the necklace below, start a peyote tube with 11ºs, as you normally would. After you step up to start the fourth row, pick up a 3mm bead and a 15º. Go back through the 3mm and pull tight to the beadwork. Pick up an 11º and go through the next protruding 11º, as usual. Add the next two 11ºs using regular tubular peyote (**illustration**).

To step up, skip the 3mm and 15º and go through the first 11º you added to the row. Stitch the next row in regular tubular peyote, adding a total of three 11ºs. Step up to start the next row, and add a picot before the first 11º, as before. Continue as before, stitching the next two stitches of this row and the next row in regular tubular peyote, then stepping up and adding the next point on the eighth row. Repeat until the piece is the desired length.

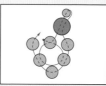

Bead Play:
Bead-stitched clasps

When finishing bead-stitched jewelry, my first choice is to use a beaded loop with a beaded toggle bar. This closure creates a seamless finish for my work. For most pieces I use the main beads that I used in the project, but there are times when beads of a contrasting type or color work even better. You will have to experiment to find out what works best for you. I would love to design and make a necklace that is constructed entirely out of toggles. Hmmmm . . .

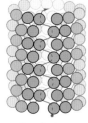

**zipping up
peyote**

*Caution! The
beads in the
toggle bar will
be tight. Be
careful not to
break a bead
while you are
securing it to
the beadwork.*

Basic peyote toggle tube

For a toggle bar about 1 in. long, pick up 18 11º beads. Work even-count peyote for 12 rows. Look at the first column. You will see how the top bead in this column is recessed while the bottom bead in this column is protruding. The top of the second column is protruding while the bottom of the second column is recessed, etc.

You will now need to form this piece of fabric into a tube by nesting the protruding and recessed beads into each other (like a zipper). Work your needle through all of the beads as they line up into each other. When you get to the end, you will meet your tail thread. I like to tie a tiny overhand knot to make sure all of the beads are tight. Weave in the tail, and weave the working thread through the beadwork to exit the middle of the tube. String a bead or two (depending on how bulky your project is), and weave the thread into the beadwork where you want to attach the toggle bar. Repeat the thread path a few times to make sure it's secure.

Beaded loops

There are two basic ways you can create the beaded loops: 1) You can bead the loop directly off of the necklace or bracelet, or 2) you can create a circle of beads separate from the necklace or bracelet and attach it after it's complete.

The beaded loop can be as simple as a circle of seed beads or as complicated as a ruffled peyote ring (see below). To make a simple peyote stitch loop, exit the project where you want the loop to sit, pick up enough beads to fit around the clasp bead or toggle, and weave the thread back into the beadwork. Exit the beadwork where you came out to begin the loop. Pick up a bead, skip the first bead on the loop, and go through the next bead. Continue around in peyote stitch, picking up a bead and skipping a bead for every stitch. The loops are very adaptable, so you can stripe them, embellish them, or just leave them plain.

Peyote ruffle and twist

Peyote twists and ruffles are created by working increases within a piece of peyote stitch fabric. When you use more beads than you need to fill in the recessed space, an overcrowding situation occurs. This overcrowding forces the piece to twist or ruffle. I use this peyote variation to add some whimsy to toggle-loop closures, but there are plenty of other applications.

Start by stringing enough beads to make a loop for the toggle. You may want to alternate colors to help you keep the beads in the right line. Work the first row in regular peyote, then work the next row by picking up two beads instead of one for every stitch. These beads will not fit, and the beadwork will start to curl. You can stop now and attach the piece to your project – the loop will lay in a nice flat circle for the toggle, as in the blue and red loop shown above. If you want a wider piece, or a more ruffled effect, keep going, adding two beads for each stitch in every row. You can also add picots, points, and other embellishments to the outside of the ring.

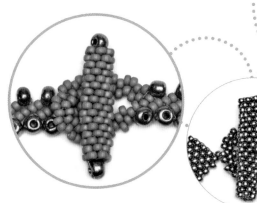

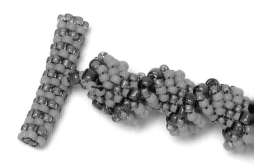

Even the basic toggle can make a classy statement. Here, matte green beads form the bar and the loop, with gold beads added to either end of the bar for decoration. If you add beads to the ends of your toggle bar, take the additional length into account when making your loop.

The tiny 15°s used in the bar and loop here make for a seamless, almost invisible finish.

Cream-lined 11°s make a simple toggle bar, but the loop makes the clasp dramatic. The first round was an alternating pattern of cubes and 11°s, with a second round of 11°s added in peyote stitch. The difference in the bead sizes helps the loop to lay flat and gives it a nice striped effect. In the center of the loop, two 11°s were added in peyote stitch to help make the turn.

Vertical striping is easy to do, and creates a dramatic effect. Alternating olive green and fuchsia gives this toggle a heavy dose of artistic color contrast, and carries on the colors in the bracelet.

Toggle Variations

Surface picots with 15°s add a delicate embellishment to a simple, solid clasp.

This eye-catching clasp uses cylinder beads for the toggle bar and the first three rows of the bead loop. The fourth, fifth, and sixth rows of the loop use two 15°s for each stitch, and the last round adds an embellishment of hex-cut points around the circumference. It's dramatic, but the colors keep it subtle.

For high-contrast color and texture, this clasp uses a geometric pattern of black, white, and red on the toggle and the loop. The embellishment at the edge makes the ruffle seem bigger than it is.

Brick Stitch

chapter 2

Brick stitch is fairly easy to learn – the beads "lock" together to make a sturdy fabric, even with beads of different sizes and shapes. I love to use a variety of beads in long, twisted brick stitch chains. Plus, it's easy to combine brick stitch with other stitches, like peyote. Sounds like brick stitch may be the perfect stitch, right? Only if you're long on patience, as brick stitch is a slow stitch. Stitching each bead into place takes a while, which is why I usually stick to brick stitch chains or use brick stitch in combination with other stitches. Nonetheless, it's a wonderful stitch to learn, with plenty of creative options.

Remember the illustration of the brick wall from Chapter 1? The one we turned on its side to illustrate peyote stitch?

Now turn it back to look like a brick wall and you will have the perfect illustration for brick stitch.

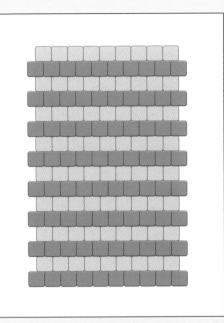

Brick stitch is worked horizontally from this position, in perfectly straight lines. The work "grows" by stacking more bricks (just like building a wall). You can create stripes horizontally …

as well as diagonally …

but not vertically.

The flat sides (top and bottom here) are the "working" sides and the protruding/recessed (right and left sides here) are the non-working sides.

BASIC BRICK STITCH

Although brick stitch looks a lot like peyote, it's made in a very different way. One unique quality of brick stitch is that you don't start the first row with brick stitch. Instead, there are two starts you can try: stitching a "ladder" of beads for the first row, or stitching a column of two-bead-wide peyote, which becomes the first two rows. I prefer the two-bead-wide peyote stitch start because it's faster, but many projects must start with the single-row ladder, so I've included them both.

Ladder stitch start

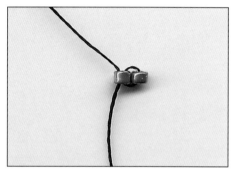 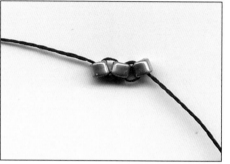 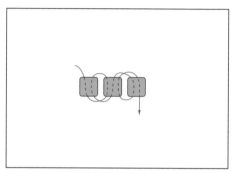

Start by picking up two beads, and pass the needle back through the first bead in the same direction. The thread will form a circle, with the two beads sitting side by side.

Go through the second bead again, and pick up the third bead. Circle back through beads #2 and 3 again in the same direction.

Continue adding beads in this manner until you have reached your desired width, then start the next row using brick stitch.

Two-bead-wide peyote start

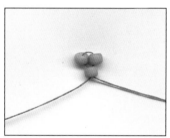 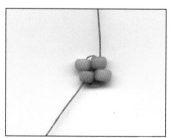 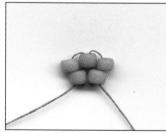 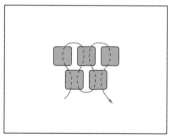

Pick up three beads. Skip beads #3 and #2 and go back through bead #1 in the opposite direction. Both the thread tail and working thread should be coming out of the bead in the same direction.

Pick up bead #4 and pass your needle back through bead #3.

Pick up bead #5 and pass your needle back through bead #4.

Continue adding beads until you reach your desired width. You have the first two rows of your piece and will begin brick stitch with the third row.

Simple Striped Ring

This cute little ring is a great first brick stitch project. I like to keep my brick-stitch projects fast and easy, but if you're ambitious, you can turn this ring into a bracelet very easily – just keep stitching until the band fits around your wrist and add a clasp.

1. Using 12 color A beads and following the instructions for the two-bead-wide peyote start, stitch two rows of six beads each (**photo a**).

2. Pick up two color B beads. Working from back to front, put the needle under the thread bridge between the last two beads (**photo b**). Sew back up into the second color B bead, locking the beads in place (**photo c**).

3. Pick up a color B bead. Going from back to front, put your needle under the next thread bridge on the previous row. Go back up the second bead just added to lock it in place (**photo d**).

4. Continue down the row, picking up a bead, going under the next thread bridge, and going back up the bead for three more stitches.

5. Repeat steps 2–4 with color B beads to stitch the next row. Remember that each new row begins with two beads. Lock the stitch in place by going back up through the second bead.

6. Continue working brick stitch, alternating two rows of As with two rows of Bs (or any striping pattern that pleases you) until the band fits around your finger. My ring is 40 rows long.

7. To finish the ring, bend the band into a circle. With your needle coming out of an end bead on the last row, sew through the first bead of the first row, turn, and sew back through the second bead of the first row. Then, go under the thread bridge between the first two beads in the last row (**photo e**).

8. Go back through the second bead of the first row (**photo f**). Pull the ring together tightly. You are doing brick stitch, but not adding any new beads.

9. Go back through the third bead in the first row, and under the thread bridge between the second and third bead in the last row. Go back up the third bead in the first row.

10. Continue stitching the ends together until the entire row is sewn together. Weave in the ends and trim.

MATERIALS:
- 11º Japanese seed beads, color A
- 11º Japanese seed beads, color B
- beading thread
- size 10 or 12 beading needle

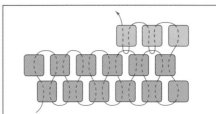

beginning row 3

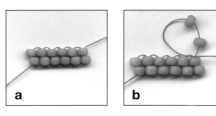

a

b

c

d

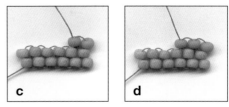

e

f

Brick stitch chain

You can make brick stitch rows as wide as you like, or as narrow as two beads. I love making simple two-bead-per-row chains. They work up quickly, and with brick stitch I can use a wide variety of beads.

To make the two-bead chain, pick up two beads and go through them both again, so that the thread makes a circle and the beads sit side by side. Pick up two beads, go under the thread bridge between the first two beads, and go back up the last bead picked up. Repeat until the chain is the desired length, picking up two beads per row, and going under the thread bridge and up the last bead added. This bracelet alternates two rows of 8ºs with one row of 4mm cube beads.

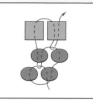

Alternating brick stitch chain

Instead of making rows of a single type of bead, you can use two different beads in each row to make an alternating chain. I like to use 11ºs with triangle beads or pearls, but the possibilities abound. You can even vary the number of beads per stitch for different looks.

For a simple alternating chain, pick up two 11ºs and one 8º. Go through the two 11ºs again to form a circle. The working thread and the tail come out opposite sides of the two 11ºs (**photo a**).

Pick up an 8º and two 11ºs. Working from back to front, put your needle under the thread bridge between the 8º and 11ºs on the first row and go back up the two 11ºs (**photo b**). Repeat, picking up an 8º and two 11ºs for each stitch, until you've reached your desired length.

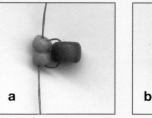

a   b

Twisted brick stitch

In basic brick stitch and brick stitch chains, after you add the two beads that start (or comprise) the row, you go under the thread bridge and back up the last bead you picked up to lock the beads in place. While making a brick stitch chain, I accidentally locked the stitch by going back into the first bead that I picked up for the row, instead of the last. Through that lucky mistake, twisted brick stitch was born! I love the texture I get when I use different beads for each row, and the way I can accentuate the spiral using different shapes and colors. Many of my chains have 10–12 different beads.

Twisted Brick Stitch Necklace

Using two different beads per row allows you to create columns of beads that gently spiral around each other. Try using beads that are about the same size, but different shapes or colors.

1. Pick up one 8º seed bead and one hex-cut seed bead. Go back into the 8º in the same direction to create a circle with the thread. The tail thread and the working thread will be coming out of two different sides of the 8º, and the beads will sit side by side (**photo a**).

2. Pick up an 8º and a hex-cut. Working from the back to the front, sew under the thread bridge between the two beads below (**photo b**).

3. Sew up the first bead of row 2, the 8º – not the second bead, the hex-cut, as you normally would with brick stitch (**photo c**).

4. Pick up an 8º and a hex-cut. Working back to front, sew under the thread bridge between the two row 2 beads and back up through the first bead of row 3 (**photo d**). Repeat until the chain is the desired length, and finish as desired.

This chain will start to twist very quickly. To ensure that you sew under the thread bridge of the previous row from back to front every time, make sure the 8º is on the left and the hex-cut is on the right.

MATERIALS:
- 8º Japanese seed beads
- 8º hex-cut seed beads
- beading thread
- size 10 or 12 beading needle

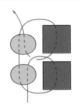

twisted brick stitch

a

b

c

d

Bead Play:
Brick and peyote

Peyote and brick stitch look so much alike, it's hard to tell which stitch is which unless you take them apart. Each stitch has its advantages: Peyote works up very quickly, while brick is super adaptable. You get the best of both worlds when you combine the two stitches.

Brick stitch on the diagonal

While this stitch resembles diagonal peyote, the process is very different and allows for a great deal of freedom combining beads of different sizes and shapes. I use this technique to make bracelets, rings, earrings, and bead-drop strap necklaces. You can use any number of beads for the width, and then work the stitch for any number of rows. This pair of earrings uses a pattern six beads wide and four rows high.

PROJECT
Brick/Peyote Earrings

1. Use the two-bead-wide peyote start (p. 34) until you have two rows of six beads each.

2. Work in brick stitch for two more rows, for a total of four rows (**photo a**).

3. Work the next row in brick stitch for only three beads (**photo b**).

4. Work three more rows using only three beads for each row.

5. Using peyote stitch, pick up a bead and go through the protruding bead in the previous row (**photo c**). Pick up another bead, and work another peyote stitch (**photo d**).

6. Turn, and make two peyote stitches, back to the last row (**photo e**). Turn, and work two peyote stitches down the row, then two stitches back up. You should have a total of six beads on the top row, with the needle coming out of the last bead of the top row (**photo f**).

7. Repeat steps 3–6 to add another section to the chain (**photo g**).

8. Exiting the last bead of the last row, pick up three cylinder beads, a pearl, and two cylinders. Go back through the first cylinder and weave the thread into the beadwork.

9. Thread a needle on the tail where you began the earring. Pick up a cylinder, the loop of an earring finding, and a cylinder. Weave into the beadwork to form a loop. Trim the tails.

10. Make a second earring like the first. When you attach the earring finding, make sure the earrings hang as mirror images of each other.

MATERIALS:
- Japanese cylinder beads
- 2 top-drilled pearls
- pair of earring findings
- beading thread
- size 10 or 12 beading needle

 a

 b

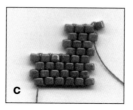 c

 d

 e

 f

 g

Other Possibilities with Diagonal Brick Stitch

This elegant ring alternates patches of 15º nickel-colored seed beads with 3mm freshwater pearls. Using diagonal brick stitch makes it easy to combine the different types of beads.

The dramatic zigzag of this ring band (made using patches of eight-bead columns by six-bead rows, with an additional four-by-six patch) complements the two-hole freshwater pearl centerpiece.

This playful bracelet was made using beads of different sizes and colors to make a colorful striped pattern. I finished this with a simple beaded toggle-and-loop clasp.

Odd-count peyote patches

In Chapter 1, I mentioned that even-count peyote has no single center column of beads. If you look back at the diagram of peyote (the brick wall turned on its side) you will remember that the protruding/recessed sides (top and bottom) are the "working sides," and the flat sides on the left and right are the "non-working" sides. These non-working sides are a perfect base for brick stitch. If you want to create a piece of peyote stitched fabric that has a center column, you can simply work your pattern in even-count peyote (you will have to ignore the last column in the pattern for now) and then add the last column using brick stitch.

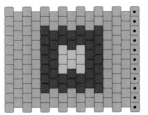

Looking at the diagram you'll see that the patch consists of 15 total columns. Ignore the last blue column of beads (the ones with the black dots) for now, and work a patch of 14 columns in even-count peyote. Once you've finished the patch, weave through the beadwork to exit an end bead on the non-working side, and add the extra column using brick stitch. To add the final bead, you'll need to sew under the same thread bridge you sewed under when you attached the second-to-last bead. In my opinion, this is easier than stitching odd-count peyote, which has an unusual turn on one side. You could make this entirely in brick stitch, but I think peyote works up much faster.

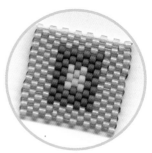

I enjoy this technique so much, I made seven peyote patches and sewed them together to make the bracelet above. The patches started out as class samples when I was teaching this technique, and while I was working on a square beaded clasp, I had the idea to stitch them all together into one bracelet. My mom liked this bracelet so much I had to make her one of her own.

This easy, versatile stitch creates a fabric of beads that is flexible in all directions. Right-angle weave is also very adaptable, making it easy to change the number of beads used in each stitch, allowing many different effects. The basic concept behind right-angle weave is to create small square rings of beads that flow one into the next. The name comes from the shape of the stitch – each new bead is added at a right angle to the bead before.

Right-Angle Weave

chapter 3

While right-angle weave is fairly easy to master, I find it a bit tricky to teach. I once taught a class on right-angle weave at a bead store, and the students were not catching on to my instructions as quickly as I had hoped. The owner of the store happened to be on the phone with master beader Jeannette Cook, who shared her right-angle weave teaching technique with me. I passed along her information to my students and after a few more attempts, the students had that magical "aha" moment. Jeannette was kind enough to allow me to share her apartment building analogy here.

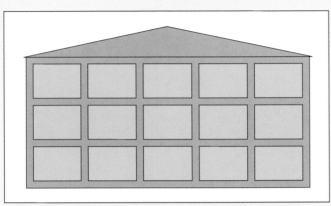

Picture a multilevel apartment building. Each apartment has a floor, a ceiling, and two walls. All but the first and last units of each floor share two common walls. The floor of one apartment is the ceiling of the one below.

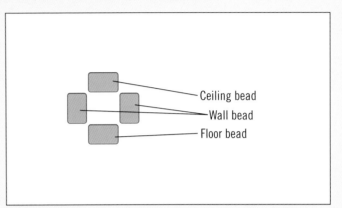

A unit of right-angle weave is much like an apartment in this building. The ceiling bead sits at the top, the floor bead is at the bottom, and the two wall beads are on each side. Notice how all the beads sit at right angles to each other?

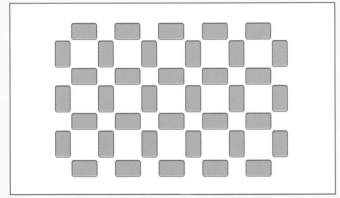

As you create the bead fabric, you'll see that each unit shares wall beads with units on either side, and the floor bead of one unit is the ceiling bead of the one below. You build right-angle weave one row, or floor, at a time.

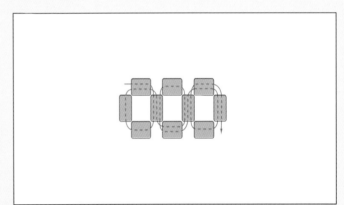

Each apartment, or unit, is added by weaving through the beads in a circular motion. As you add each subsequent unit, you'll switch the direction in which you're beading. The first unit you'll stitch going clockwise around the ring, then the next unit you'll add stitching counterclockwise. Remember, every bead you add will be at a right angle to the bead you just went through.

If you use beads with large holes, you'll get a better tension if you use doubled thread. Because you switch direction as you bead, your beads might not sit at right angles to each other. Don't worry – this is part of the charm of right-angle weave. Look at this sample I made. The beads don't sit at exact right angles to each other, but you can still see each bead unit clearly.

BASIC RIGHT-ANGLE WEAVE

The beads you use in right-angle weave affect the look of the weave. Beads like cubes, hex-cuts, and cylinders, which are more rectangular than Czech or Japanese seed beads, will lock together into the square shape of the pattern easily, while the rounder seed beads will form more circular rings and show less thread.

For this demonstration, I used cube beads, which really show the angles of the stitch. Start by stringing four beads. Go back through all four beads and tie the working thread to the tail. Pass your needle through the bead next to the knot. The threads will be coming out of opposite sides of the same bead.

Do you see the ceiling bead at the top, the floor bead at the bottom and the two wall beads? Turn the beads so that the threads are coming out of the ceiling bead. Pass your needle through the wall bead to get ready to add the next "apartment," or ring of beads, which will share a wall with this one.

Pick up three new beads. Pass your needle back down through the adjoining wall bead from the first apartment to secure the stitch.

Pass your needle through the floor bead and up the new wall bead. You are now ready to build the next apartment.

Pick up three beads. Pass your needle back up through the adjoining wall bead to secure the stitch, then go through the ceiling bead and the new wall bead.

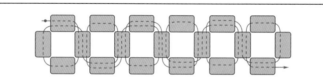

Continue across the row, building apartments, until you have six rings completed. Do not pass your needle up the last wall. You thread should be coming out of a floor bead.

This floor bead will now be the ceiling of the next level of apartments.

Pick up three beads and go back through the ceiling bead.

Pass your needle down the outside wall bead, through the floor bead, up the inside wall bead, and through the ceiling bead of the next apartment. You are now ready for the next stitch.

Pick up two beads. (You're adding a wall bead and a floor bead, since you already have the ceiling and one wall of this apartment.) Go up through the adjoining wall bead, through the ceiling bead, and down the new wall bead.

Pick up two beads. Go through the ceiling bead of the next apartment, down the adjoining wall bead, through the floor bead, up the new wall bead, and through the ceiling bead of the next apartment.

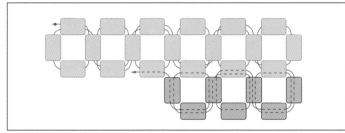

If you have trouble keeping track of which way to go when you add beads, remember that one stitch is done in a clockwise direction while the next stitch is done in a counterclockwise direction.

Continue adding apartments until you reach the end of the row. Go through the floor bead of the last apartment to get into position to start the next row. This floor bead will become the ceiling bead of the next apartment.

Pick up three new beads, and go through the ceiling bead. Go through the wall bead to get into position to start the next apartment.

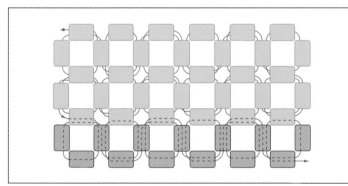

Work in right-angle weave, adding two beads per stitch, until you reach the end of the row. Then, continue working in right-angle weave until you've reached the desired length.

Right-angle weave patches

I made this colorful bracelet of offset patches by adding a column of units to one side, and omitting a column from the other side. First, I did five rows of four apartments. At the end of the fifth row, instead of weaving down through the floor bead to start the next row, I picked up three black beads and went through the wall bead again. Then I went down through the floor bead of the new unit and started the new row there, with a different color. I made four apartments across, stopping one unit short of the end of the row above, and started the next row. At the end of the fifth row of this color, I added a new column to the other side the same way. The result was this fun, alternating patch bracelet.

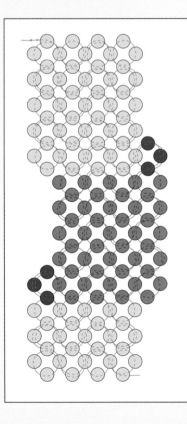

MATERIALS:
- 11º seed beads, mixed colors
- beading thread
- size 10 or 12 beading needle

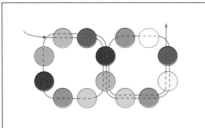

clasp loop

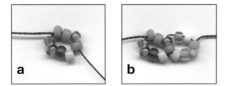

a

b

c

d

e

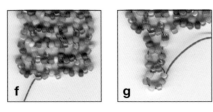

f

g

Right-Angle-Weave Bracelet — A Seed Bead Challenge

The pattern for this bracelet is a little more open than basic right-angle weave. For each unit you will use eight beads instead of four.

1. Pick up eight beads, and go through them again. Tie the working thread to the tail with a square knot. Continue through the next four beads, so that your thread comes out of the bottom of a wall bead (**photo a**).

2. Pick up six beads. Go back down through the two adjoining wall beads, and through the floor and new wall beads (**photo b**).

3. Continue in right-angle weave, forming eight-bead apartments, until your row is five units long. Pass your needle through the two floor beads to begin the next row (**photo c**).

4. Pick up six beads. Go through the ceiling beads again (these were the floor beads of the apartment above). Pass your needle down the new inside wall beads to begin the next stitch (**photo d**).

5. Pick up four beads. Go through the ceiling beads, down the adjoining wall beads, and through the floor beads. Continue up the new wall beads and through the ceiling beads of the next apartment (**photo e**).

6. Continue in right-angle weave until your bracelet just fits around your wrist.

7. To stitch the finishing loop, carefully sew through the beadwork (work in circles to avoid crossing through the centers of the apartments) until your thread is coming out of the floor beads of the second apartment from the end, pointing toward the outside of the bracelet (**photo f**).

8. Pick up six beads and go back through the floor beads and the next four beads. Repeat twice to make a total of three units, and bring your needle up the new wall beads (**photo g**).

9. Pick up six beads and create a unit by going back up the wall beads. Continue through the ceiling beads and back down the new wall beads (**photo h**).

10. Create another apartment by picking up six beads and going back down the new wall. Continue through the next six beads, coming out the ceiling beads.

11. Pick up six beads for the next apartment. Go through the two ceiling beads from the last unit, and through the next four beads.

12. To finish the loop, pick up two wall beads. Pass your needle through the two floor beads in the second apartment of the bracelet (they will form the ceiling of this unit). Pick up the other two wall beads and go though the two floor beads. Weave in the ends.

13. Attach a toggle (see p. 30) or button to the other end of the bracelet, using the tail thread (**photo i**).

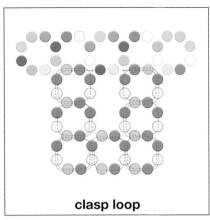

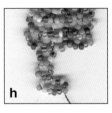

clasp loop

DOUBLE-DECK RIGHT-ANGLE WEAVE

While working with diagonal peyote, I wondered what other stitches I could work diagonally. I tried my hand at working right-angle weave on the diagonal, but I didn't like my first attempt because it came out wobbly and somewhat formless. I kept playing with it, however, and eventually came up with something I liked. I call this stitch double-deck right-angle weave because of the two distinct layers in the initial chain. It just goes to show what wonderful unexpected results you can get when you play around!

Start double-deck right-angle weave as you would normal right-angle weave: Make a ring of four beads. Go through the ceiling bead and down the wall bead, and pick up three beads. Go through the adjoining wall bead again, and continue through the floor bead.

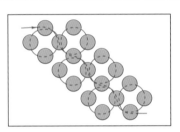

Instead of going up the other wall and picking up three new beads, you're now going to create a new row of apartments. The floor bead you are coming out of will be the ceiling bead of the first new apartment. Pick up three beads, and go back through the ceiling bead and down the wall bead. Now you'll add the apartment next door by picking up three beads and going through the adjoining wall bead. Continue through the floor bead. This bead will become the ceiling bead of the next row. Add the next two apartments just like the last two. Continue making the chain until you've reached your desired length, and exit a floor bead.

Turn the chain to sit horizontally, with the working thread on the right. Notice how the beads in each row are arranged in pairs. There is a definite space between these pairs. Continuing with the working thread, go through both beads in the first pair, and the first bead of the second pair.

Pick up two beads and go through the last bead of the first pair and the first bead of the second pair in the same direction, making a ring. Go through the next two beads in the row (the second bead of the second pair and the first bead of the next pair). Pick up two more beads and go through the two beads you went through last in the previous row.

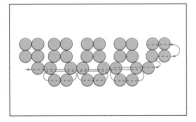

Continue across the row until you reach the end of the chain. You can add another row of beads the same way, if you like. This chain looks great made with a single type of bead or with a wide variety of colors, shapes, and sizes.

Nona Collar

When I made this necklace it reminded me of the daughter of a friend of mine. So I now call it "Nona."

1. Pick up two blue beads and two hex-cut beads. Create a circle by going back through the two blue beads (**photo a**).

2. Pick up one blue bead and two green beads. Create a circle by going back through the last blue bead from the previous stitch and the new blue bead you just picked up (**photo b**).

3. Pick up one blue bead and two hex-cuts. Create a circle by going back through the last blue bead from the previous stitch and the new blue bead you just picked up (**photo c**). Notice how the green beads and the hex-cuts fall on opposite sides of the blue beads.

4. Repeat steps 2 and 3 until you have reached your desired length. Remember that a clasp will add length. End with a stitch using hex-cuts. To start the next row, pass your needle down through the last hex-cut added.

MATERIALS:
- 11º beads, color A (blue)
- 11º beads, color B (green)
- 11º Japanese hex-cut beads
- 8º triangle beads
- beading thread
- size 10 or 12 beading needle

5. Go through the next two hex-cuts (the second bead of the first pair and the first bead of the second pair). Pick up two green beads. Go through the two hex-cuts again to make a circle (**photo d**).

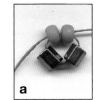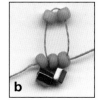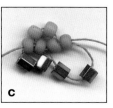
a   b   c

6. Pass your needle through the next two hex-cuts. Pick up two green beads and go through the hex-cuts again to make another circle. Repeat until you reach the end of the row. To get ready for the next row, go down through the last green bead added in the bottom row.

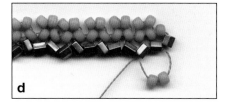
d

7. Go through the next two green beads, the second bead of the first pair and the first bead of the second pair, as on the prior row (**photo e**).

8. Pick up one triangle bead. Create a circle by going through the two green beads again (**photo f**). Go through the next two green beads, and repeat with another triangle. Continue across the row until you reach the end.

e

9. Weave in the threads and attach a clasp as desired. I used a handmade toggle clasp with a stick pearl as the bar for my necklace. When I stitched this necklace I accidentally made it too short. To solve this problem, I stitched an extender section using daisy chain (see Chapter 5). Problem solved.

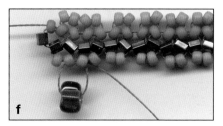
f

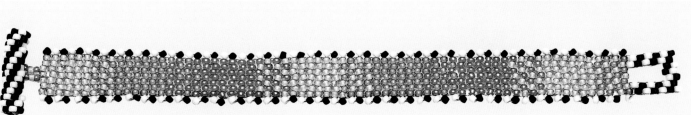

Pebble stitch

This variation looks like a brand new stitch, but it's done the same way as double-deck right-angle weave. Standard double-deck is stitched horizontally, with long rows stitched from one end of the project to the other. With this "pebble stitch" variation, the rows are much shorter and tighter and the project grows end to end, instead of top to bottom – even though it's stitched the same way! The result combines aspects of many different stitches. The fabric is beautifully supple, and I love the way the beads sit at slight angles to one another, giving the piece a textured, almost organic look.

To do this stitch, start as you would double-deck right-angle weave: Pick up four beads and make a ring by going through the first two beads again. Pick up three beads, and go though the second bead picked up for the first apartment and the first of the three new beads. Pick up three new beads and go through the first bead picked up for the second apartment and the first of the three new beads. Continue until you have eight apartments.

Stitch the next row as typical double-deck right-angle weave. Then stitch the next row the same way. That's it! Just keep stitching rows of double-deck until you reach the desired length.

The key to this stitch is tension, particularly in the first two rows. You have to make sure your loops are tight, or you'll end up with gaps and visible thread instead of columns and rows of uniformly tilted beads.

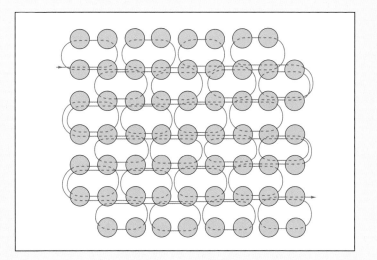

DIAGONAL RIGHT-ANGLE WEAVE

Though I was pleasantly surprised at developing my double-deck version of right-angle weave (see p. 45),
I still wanted to see if I could figure out a diagonal version of the stitch. After more frustrating attempts –
and a suggestion from bead artist Lynne Irelan – I realized that I needed to stabilize the structure of the stitch
and shift my perspective. I tried again, and my version of diagonal right-angle weave was born.

Start by picking up four beads. Leave a 10-in. tail and go through the beads again to form a circle. Tie the tail to the working thread. Go through the next bead. This will be the ceiling bead.

Go down the wall bead. Pick up three beads and form a circle by going through the adjoining wall bead. Continue through the floor bead.

The floor bead you are coming out of will now be the ceiling bead of the new apartment you are going to build. Pick up three beads. Circle back into the ceiling bead, and continue down the wall bead.

Pick up three beads and go back through the adjoining wall bead and the floor bead.

Go up the wall bead to start the next row. Pick up three beads and go up the adjoining wall bead.

Your thread is coming up the shared wall bead of the newest apartment. Go through the ceiling bead of the middle apartment on the bottom row, and then up through the wall bead of the apartment above that.

The two beads you just passed through will become the floor and wall of a new apartment. Pick up two beads and circle back through the floor and wall beads, and continue through the two beads just added.

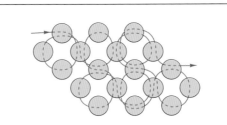

Get ready for the next stitch by going through the ceiling bead, down the wall bead, and through the ceiling bead of the last apartment in the bottom row (this will become the floor bead of the next new apartment).

Pick up two beads and circle back through the wall and floor beads. Go down the wall bead of the last bottom row apartment.

Pick up three beads. Go back down the adjoining wall bead.

You now have the same number of apartments in each row. Go through the

floor and wall beads to begin building the next bottom row apartment. Pick up three beads and go through the adjoining wall bead. Weave back up to the top of the chain, and continue as before.

Diagonal Right-Angle-Weave Bracelet

What happens to a stitch when you change the beads used? What happens when you combine two completely different beads? This bracelet happens, that's what! While I tried a number of bead combinations, I really liked the way the 8°s and the bugle beads looked together. For this bracelet, I used 8°s for the ceiling/floor beads and bugle beads for the wall beads.

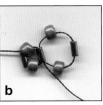

a **b**

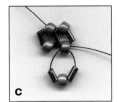
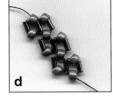

c **d**

1. Pick up one 8°, one bugle, one 8°, and one bugle. Go through all four beads again. Tie the working thread to the tail, and go through the first 8°. This bead is the ceiling bead. You should have your tail thread and your working thread coming out of both sides of this bead (**photo a**).

2. Go down the wall bead. Pick up one 8°, one bugle, and one 8°. Go back down the adjoining wall bead (**photo b**). Continue through the new floor bead to get ready for the next stitch.

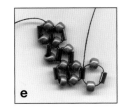
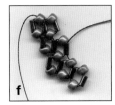

e **f**

3. Pick up one bugle, one 8°, and one bugle. Go through the ceiling bead of this new apartment (**photo c**). Continue down the new wall bead.

4. Pick up one 8°, one bugle, and one 8°. Go back down the adjoining wall bead and through the floor bead to get ready for the next row of apartments.

5. Repeat steps 3 and 4. The thread should come out of the floor bead of the last apartment you built (**photo d**).

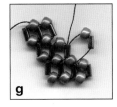
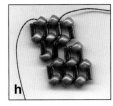

g **h**

6. Go up the wall bead. Pick up one 8°, one bugle, and one 8°. Go back up the adjoining wall bead (**photo e**).

MATERIALS:
- 8° beads
- 3mm bugle beads
- beading thread
- size 10 or 12 beading needle

7. Go through the ceiling of the adjoining apartment and up through the wall bead of the apartment above that (**photo f**).

8. Pick up one 8° and one bugle. Go back through the floor and wall beads of the new apartment (**photo g**).

9. Repeat step 7 and step 8. The thread should come up out of the adjoining wall bead in the top row (**photo h**).

10. Go through the ceiling bead and down the wall bead. Continue through the ceiling bead of the last apartment in the second row.

11. Pick up one bugle and one 8º. Go down the adjoining wall bead and the floor bead of the new apartment (**photo i**).

12. Go down the wall bead of the last second row apartment. Continue through the ceiling bead of the last apartment on the bottom row. Pick up one bugle and one 8º. Go down the adjoining wall bead and the floor bead of this new apartment (**photo j**). Go down the wall bead of the last apartment on the bottom row to get ready for the next stitch.

13. Pick up one 8º, one bugle, and one 8º. Go down the adjoining wall bead and continue through the floor bead.

14. Repeat steps 6 through 12 until you have reached your desired length. Finish as desired. I used a beaded toggle-and-loop clasp.

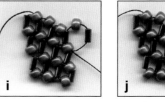

Drop beads

The basic diagonal right-angle weave strap has a beautiful drape to it, but sometimes I want to add a little more. I love adding drop beads to my strap necklaces. A version of this technique was published in the August 2006 issue of *Bead&Button* magazine, featuring top-drilled coin pearls and silver seed beads.

Here, I've used bronze seed beads and top-drilled stone beads for a contemporary look.

Start out by weaving about five or six rows of diagonal right-angle weave. Pass your needle through the floor bead of the last bottom-row apartment. Pick up enough beads to cover the space from the hole in the drop bead to the top of one side. It is usually just two or three beads. Pick up a drop bead and two or three beads to cover the other side of the drop bead. Go through the floor bead of the last apartment (**photo**).

Go up the wall bead, and continue working in diagonal right-angle weave until you are in position to add your next drop. Then, add the next drop as before. Continue until you reach your desired length.

Bead Play:
Fun beaded bag

In 1998, my first published piece – this fabulous right-angle weave pouch using thousands of "leftover" beads – appeared in *Bead&Button* magazine. I was new to right-angle weave but had decided to challenge myself.

Like the bead soup bracelet in this chapter, each apartment here uses two beads for each wall, floor, and ceiling. I made 52 apartments in each row, and stitched 33 rows. Then I added a netted edging to the bag and threaded a cord through to make a closure and a strap.

This project was time-consuming, but I love the results. Don't be afraid to take on larger projects or try something besides jewelry.

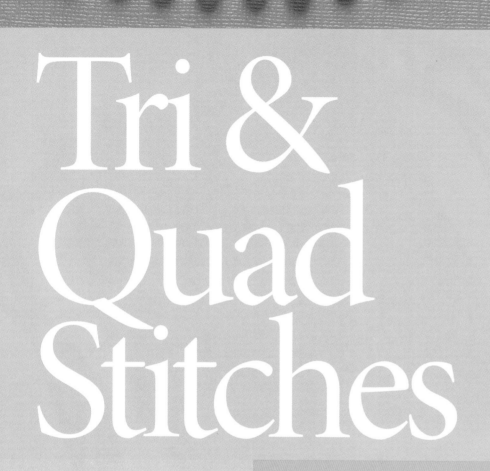

Tri & Quad Stitches

My tri and quad stitches could be considered variations of right-angle weave rather than stitches in their own right, but because they behave so differently from right-angle weave, they get their own chapter. I love these stitches for making lacy chains – especially with bead soup! Although these stitches are simple, you can create some really elegant designs.

chapter 4

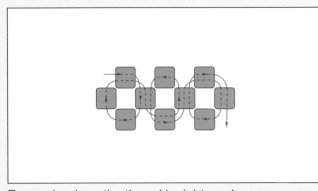

Remember how the thread in right-angle weave moved in alternating clockwise and counterclockwise circles?

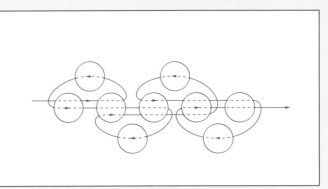

Tri stitch moves in a similar manner, but with three beads. The stitch comes together with two thread passes through the beads. First the new beads are added, then the stitch is locked into place.

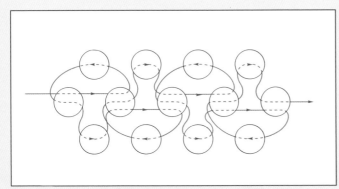

Look closely at this sample and you will see a line of angled beads running down the middle of the chain. I call these the core or center beads. The beads pointing out on either side of the chain I call the outside (or pointy) beads.

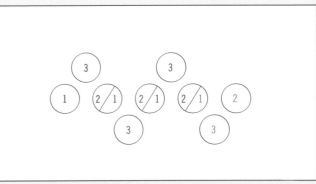

The pointy outside beads are always bead #3. These beads will alternate sides of the chain with each stitch. You will never pass back through them. The inner core beads are always your #1 and #2 beads.

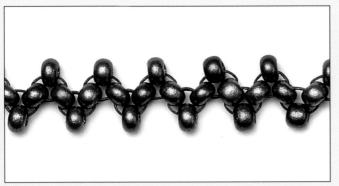

Quad stitch follows the same principle as tri stitch but adds a second bead during the second thread pass.

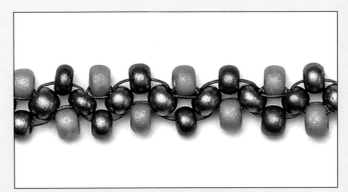

This "extra" bead stabilizes the stitch, making it easy to create long single-row chains without the twisting problems that come with right-angle weave. And it's a great stitch for working with beads of different sizes and shapes.

TRI STITCH

The stitch I call triangle stitch (tri stitch for short and to distinguish it from another stitch called triangle stitch) magically appeared one day while I was experimenting with other stitches that might work on the diagonal. As I mentioned in the last chapter, using right-angle weave did not give me what I was looking for, but it did inspire me to experiment. Instead of using four beads per stitch, I wondered what would happen if I used only three beads. I was really excited to see what was appearing in my hands.

Thinking I had invented something new, I was disappointed when, three months later, I saw this very same stitch in a magazine. The stitch was called a zigzag, and I've learned since that it's sometimes called picot stitch. I still call mine tri stitch because you go through three beads in each stitch.

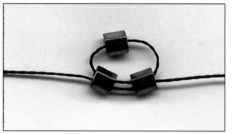

Start by picking up three seed beads. Lock the stitch in place by going through the first two beads again in the same direction. Your thread will exit the second bead, which becomes the first bead of the next three-bead stitch.

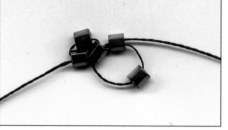

Pick up two beads (the second and third beads of the stitch). Go through the first two beads of the stitch again to lock the stitch in place.

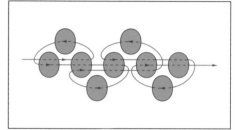

Make sure your thread is coming out of the second bead at the end of each stitch. This second bead will always become the first bead of the next stitch, and the third bead will always be the outside bead. That's it. It's that easy.

Tri stitch variations

You can create many different looks with tri stitch just by varying the beads. A simple chain of seed beads can be incredibly elegant. Try adding pearls or pairing tiny 15ºs with more robust 8ºs for something different. A chain of tri stitch using round seed beads of the same size will tend to twist as you wear it. Varying the beads can straighten the chain, hide the twist, or flaunt the curls and angles – depending on what beads you choose.

Seed beads
A simple chain of seed beads can be elegant or funky, depending on the colors you use. I love making lacy lariats with this stitch. They look classy with metallic beads and pearls, but you could make them playful with tropical or primary colors.

Mixed beads
Play with your beads and try some different combinations. Using different colors, shapes, and sizes really changes the look of tri stitch. Try using beads of different sizes for the outside points. I've used 8ºs with 11ºs and with 15ºs for two unique looks. Start by picking up two of the same beads and one different bead – two 8ºs and an 11º, for example. Go through the two 8ºs again. Pick up an 8º and an 11º, and go through the last two 8ºs again. The 11ºs will sit on the outside.

You also can use this pattern with different types of beads, as I did in my combination of 11ºs and cube beads. Because the cube beads are so much larger than the 11ºs, I used pairs of 11ºs, treating each pair as though it were a single bead.

It's very easy to pick up the "odd" bead as the third bead of every stitch, but you can also place different beads in the middle of the stitch. Try picking up an 11º, a cube, and an 11º. Go through the first 11º and the cube again, and pick up two 11ºs for the next stitch. For the

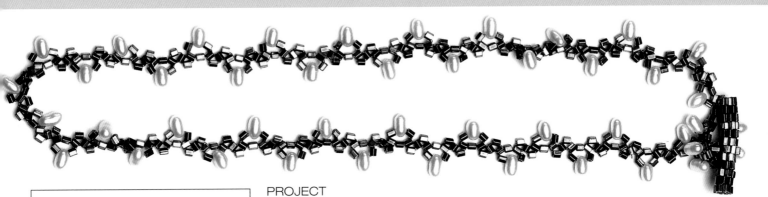

MATERIALS:
- 11º hex-cut beads
- 3mm x 5mm top-drilled pearls
- beading thread
- size 10 or 12 beading needle

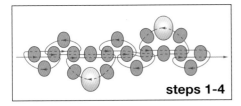

steps 1-4

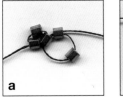 

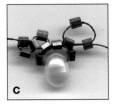 

a

b

c

d

PROJECT
Tri Stitch Necklace with Pearls

This delicate tri stitch chain uses 11º hex-cut beads and features beautiful top-drilled pearls alternating down the sides of the chain. The result is a delicate necklace perfect for casual wear or a special night out.

1. Pick up three 11º hex-cut beads. Create a ring by going back through the first two beads. Your needle is coming out of the second bead, which will become the first bead of the next stitch. Pick up two hex-cuts, and go through the first two beads of the second stitch to lock it in place (**photo a**).

2. Pick up three hex-cuts, one pearl, and one hex-cut. (The unusual number of beads helps the pearl sit between the hex-cuts without bunching up the beads.) To lock the stitch, go through the first three beads of the stitch again (**photo b**).

3. With your needle coming out of the new first bead, pick up two hex-cuts for the next stitch, and go through the first two beads of the stitch again (**photo c**). Repeat to make another stitch.

4. Repeat step 2 to make another pearl-point stitch (**photo d**), then repeat step 3. Continue until the chain is the desired length.

5. Tie off the threads and finish as desired. I added a beaded toggle-and-loop clasp to this necklace, and I love the effect of incorporating pearls into the loop.

next stitch, pick up a cube and an 11º. Alternate picking up 11º s and cubes for the second bead of each stitch, and you'll get an interesting pattern.

One of my favorite effects is the fun texture and color combinations of bead soup. Whether you use leftover beads, or a carefully blended mix, the result can be extraordinary.

Shaped beads
Using beads with geometric shapes, such as triangle beads or bugles, gives tri stitch a different look. It's still lacy, but there's a modern edge and sharper lines. Bugles and cube beads make very sturdy chains.

QUAD STITCH

And then there were four (again).

While teaching my then-10-year-old daughter how to do tri stitch, she made a mistake. She handed me her "mistake" to fix and, after taking one look at it, I said, "I think you made up a new stitch. How did you do that?" She smiled and told me that after she went through the first bead again, she added an extra bead before going through the second bead to finish the stitch. And with that, quad stitch was born. I loved her mistake and use it for many simple strap necklaces using a variety of beads.

There is one tiny drawback to this stitch, however. In the off-loom bead-stitching world, visible thread is one of the big no-nos – there should never be any exposed thread crossing over or under beads. Quad stitch has an exposed thread under the "extra" bead, but it is almost impossible to see it. For the beading purists out there, you can achieve a similar look with a single line of right-angle weave using four beads for each unit. However, quad stitch allows for a better fit of the beads when working with beads of many different sizes. Also, quad stitch seems to be more stable than a single row of right-angle weave – quad stitch doesn't twist the way right-angle weave does.

Quad stitch is very similar to tri stitch, except for the addition of an extra bead. Start by picking up three beads and going through the first bead again.

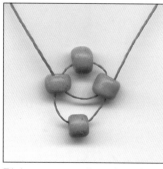

Pick up a new bead and go through the second bead to lock the stitch. The second bead becomes the first bead of the next stitch, as in tri stitch.

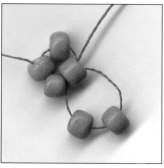

To do the second stitch, pick up two beads. Go through the first bead, pick up a new bead, and go through the second bead. Repeat to make the next stitch.

Quad stitch variations

Like tri stitch, quad stitch is a great stitch for experimentation. The beads lock together to make a sturdy chain, even with beads that are very different shapes and sizes. So feel free to go crazy.

Mixed beads

For bead-soup chains, it doesn't get much easier than this. Whether you mix all your leftovers together for a colorful and eclectic assortment, or you stick to a range of hues, almost any bead mix you like can be incorporated into your quad stitch chain.

Patterns

While I must admit that I prefer the look of this stitch using a mixture of beads in different shapes and sizes, I do like the look of simple patterns as well.

A basic pattern starts with uniform beads of one size, such as 11º s. Make the first stitch with four 11º s, then pick up an 11º and a different bead, such as a cube. Go through the first bead, pick up another cube, and go through the second bead. Make the next stitch with three new 11º s. The stitch after that you can make using beads of a different color or shape for the third and fourth beads. You can make the pattern as simple or as varied as you like.

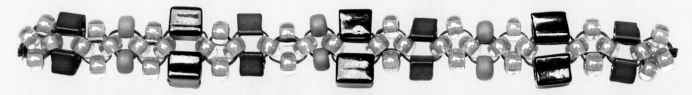

Bead Play:
Tri/Quad combination

As I became more acquainted with these stitches, I was excited to have more options. This elegant necklace combines tri stitch with quad stitch using bronze seed beads and gorgeous green top-drilled freshwater pearls. The tightness of the stitch, combined with the lacy feel, make this a great stitch for projects with multiple stitches.

This variation uses cylinder beads and longer spaces between the pearls.

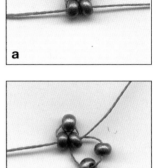

a

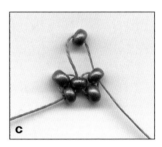

b

c

PROJECT
Delicate Pearl Chain

1. Pick up three 11ºs and circle back through the first two beads (**photo a**).

2. Pick up two 11ºs and sew back through the first 11º of the new stitch (**photo b**).

3. Pick up an 11º and continue through the second 11º of the stitch to complete a quad stitch (**photo c**).

4. Pick up two 11ºs and go through the first two 11ºs of the stitch again (**photo d**).

5. Now it's time to add a pearl. The number of 11ºs that I use to get around the top of these pearls may differ from the number you will need.

With your needle coming out of the first bead of the stitch, pick up four 11ºs, a pearl, and an 11º. Complete the stitch, circling back through the first 11º and the next three 11ºs (**photo e**). (Here, the first two 11ºs I picked up span the top of the pearl – you may need

three beads. The next 11º will actually be the first 11º of the next stitch.)

6. Pick up two 11ºs. Go through beads #1 and 2 of this stitch (**photo f**). Notice that bead #1 is the third 11º you picked up with the previous stitch.

7. Repeat steps 2–6 until you have reached your desired length.

8. Finish the necklace as you like. I used a beaded toggle and loop. I love how the top-drilled pearls fit in the loop.

MATERIALS:
- 11º seed beads
- top-drilled freshwater pearls
- beading thread
- size 10 or 12 beading needle

d

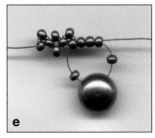

e

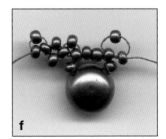

f

Daisy chain is the first beading stitch I ever learned. I remember sitting for hours in my backyard making necklaces and rings, using all of the bead colors that were available at the time. Everyone I knew was the recipient of one of my creations. At sleep-away camp I'd sit on my bed, making my own needles out of wire and beading until it was too dark to see.

As the years went by and I began to teach myself all of the off-loom beading stitches, I never once used this old childhood favorite. It never crossed my mind that this simple stitch could "grow up" just like I had. Then, while looking through a book one day in search of inspiration, I came across a picture of a daisy chain. Nothing fancy, just a basic chain, but I thought it would be fun to teach to my daughters. It was, and I rediscovered a stitch that is easy, pretty, and versatile.

Daisy Chain

chapter 5

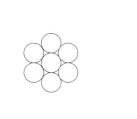

Basic daisy chain has six beads going around the outside of the stitch. When a bead is added to the center, you can see how the six outside beads make the "petals" of the daisy that gives the stitch its name.

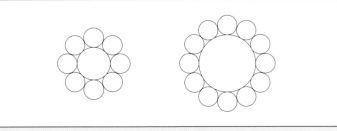

If you like, you can change the outside bead count, but you will usually have to change the size of the inside bead as well.

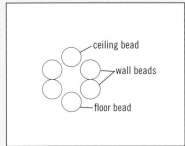

I am going to use Jeannette Cook's apartment analogy (see Chapter 3) for this stitch, too. If you look at the picture, you can see that there is one bead for the ceiling and one for the floor, and there are two beads for each of the two walls.

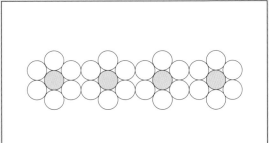

As in right-angle weave, the walls of each daisy chain stitch are shared by the next stitch.

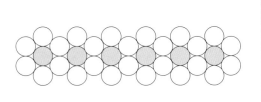

With just a little modification, you can stitch a chain with the daisies separated instead of joined ...

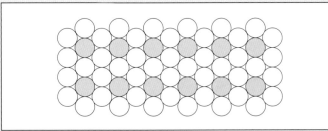

or create multiple rows of daisies ...

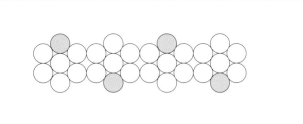

or move the center of the daisy to the outside of the stitch.

BASIC DAISY CHAIN

Traditionally, each daisy chain stitch is a circle of beads surrounding a bead of a different color, but I frequently stitch monochromatic chains. As each daisy is stitched to the next, a chain of daisies forms. Six-bead daisy chain is the most basic variety, but you can change the bead sizes and counts to almost anything.

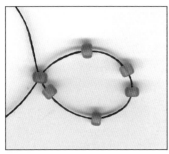 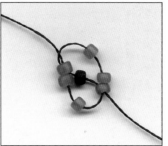  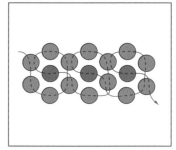

To start a basic daisy chain, pick up six beads and create a circle by going through the first bead again. You should be able to see the ceiling and floor beads, with two wall beads on each side. Position the unit so the needle is coming out between the two wall beads on the left.

Pick up one bead in a second color. Secure the bead by passing your needle down through the bottom bead of the opposite wall, so the needle comes out below the second wall bead.

The wall beads will be shared by the next apartment, so you already have two of the six beads needed for the next stitch. Pick up four beads in the first color. Create a circle by going back through the top wall bead on the right side of the first unit.

Pick up a bead in the second color, and go down through the new bottom wall bead on the right, as you did before. Continue making daisy units the same way until your chain is the desired length.

Daisy variations

With just a single chain of daisies, you can do so much. Add sparkle and luster with metal and pearls or playfulness with dangles. Make your daisies a seamless band or separate the units to make them stand out. That favorite childhood stitch is all grown up, but it can still have a bit of whimsy.

Different bead counts

Creating a daisy chain with a different number of beads around the outside is fairly easy. The most basic of these variations is eight-bead daisy chain. Make this chain the same way as a six-bead daisy chain, but use two beads for the floor and ceiling instead of one. Since the circle of beads is larger, you will need to use either a larger bead or two smaller beads in the center. Both options go a long way to change the look of the stitch. These two rings are stitched with variations on basic daisy chain. For the monochromatic ring, I used metallic cylinder beads in eight-count daisy chain with two beads in the center. For the pearl ring, I used 14 15°s around 2mm pearls.

PROJECT

Daisy Chain Earrings

Use two bead-count variations in one earring. You can create these elegant earrings in just a few minutes. Dress them up or dress them down.

MATERIALS:
- 9⁰ seed beads
- 4–5mm round freshwater or glass pearls
- pair of earring findings
- beading thread
- size 10 or 12 beading needle

For this project, I used two beads for each wall and four beads for the floors and ceilings of the pearl stitches. These counts may work for you, but you may need to adjust the bead counts based on your bead choices.

1. Pick up four seed beads and create a circle by going back through all four beads again. Tie an overhand knot here to keep the beads together. This will be the loop for the earring finding (**photo a**).

   The last two beads you passed through make up one wall of the next stitch. Remember that each wall is always made up of just two beads. In order to have enough beads to go around the circumference of the pearls, you will add beads to the ceiling and the floor.

2. Pick up ten seed beads. If you need to add or subtract beads to fit around your pearl, make sure you are using an even number. Because two of the wall beads are shared with the previous unit, I needed ten more beads to fit around my pearl.

3. Create a circle of beads by passing your needle through the top wall bead from the previous stitch (**photo b**).

4. Pick up a pearl and go down through the bottom bead of the opposite wall (**photo c**). You should have four beads each for the ceiling and the floor.

5. With your needle once again coming out of the bottom wall bead, pick up six beads and create a circle by going through the top wall bead from the previous stitch (**photo d**).

6. Pick up two beads. Go through the bottom wall bead on the opposite side of the unit (**photo e**). The ceiling and floor each have two beads.

7. Repeat steps 2 through 6 until you have a total of five pearl sections and four non-pearl sections.

8. To finish the thread, don't pick up any new beads, but continue through the floor beads, back up the opposite wall beads, and through the ceiling beads of the last apartment. Continue following the thread path for a few more beads to secure. Secure the tails, and trim.

9. Open the loop of an earring finding and attach it to the four-bead loop on the earring. Repeat all the steps to make the other earring.

Here's an idea – forget the earrings! Use this same pattern to make a fabulous bracelet or keep working to make a choker.

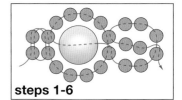

steps 1-6

a

b

c

d

e

Stand-alone daisies

You can make each of your daisies stand alone, without sharing walls, by adding a slight modification to your daisy chain. After adding your center bead and completing the stitch, pick up two beads (essentially the wall beads of the next stitch), circle back down the wall beads of the existing stitch, and go up the new wall beads to secure.

Adding dangles

You have probably figured out that I love the look of embellished strap necklaces. You can add all sorts of drops to a daisy chain, and there are three basic ways to do it.

Vertically drilled dangles

With your needle coming out of the bottom wall bead of the previous daisy, pick up three seed beads, one drop bead, and one more seed bead. Skip the last seed bead strung, pass your needle back up the drop bead, and continue through the next two seed beads. Pick up four more seed beads. Pass your needle through the top wall bead to create the circle. Complete the stitch by picking up one seed bead and going through the bottom wall bead on the opposite side (**illustration a**).

Top-drilled dangles

Top-drilled dangles, such as briolettes or pearls, are done a little differently. To add these dangles, come out the bottom wall bead of the last completed daisy. Pick up two beads plus the number of beads needed to get you from the top of the bead to the hole (this is usually two or three more). Pick up the top-drilled pearl and two or three beads to get from the hole back to the top of the pearl. Pass the needle back through the first two beads you strung. Pick up three more seed beads. Pass the needle through the top wall bead to complete the circle. Complete the stitch by picking up one seed bead and going through the bottom wall bead on the

opposite side (**illustration b**).

You can also add top-drilled beads this way: Pick up one seed bead plus the number of seed beads needed to get you from the top of the bead to the hole. Pick up the top-drilled pearl and two or three beads to get from the hole back to the top of the pearl. Now, pass your needle back through the floor bead in the same direction (the hole in this seed bead should be going side to side instead of up and down). Pick up three more seed beads. Finish the stitch as described above (**illustration c**).

You don't need to attach every dangle the same way. When Nancy Garber from Brighton Beads and More shared a strand of fabulous multihued pearls with me, I had a lot of fun finding the best way to hang every dangle (below). The different shapes, colors, and sizes are what make this necklace so eye-catching.

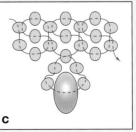

Caribbean Necklace

I love to play with color and texture in my bead designs, and this necklace is a great example of using a stitch in an unusual way. The color pattern and different bead sizes might fool you, but this is, indeed, daisy chain.

MATERIALS
- 8º Japanese seed beads (transparent light green white-lined)
- matte cylinder beads, color A (dark orange)
- matte cylinder beads, color B (turquoise blue)
- 10–20mm coordinating glass beads
- beading thread
- size 10 or 12 beading needle

1. Beginning with a green 8º, string an alternating pattern of 8ºs and blue cylinder beads three times. Go through the first bead again to make a ring (**photo a**). This will be your top left wall bead.

2. Pick up an orange cylinder bead. Pass your needle down through the bottom right wall bead (a blue cylinder) to secure (**photo b**).

3. Pick up an 8º, a blue cylinder, an 8º, and a blue cylinder. Pass your needle through the top wall bead (an 8º) to create a circle (**photo c**).

4. Repeat steps 2 and 3 until you have completed three complete stitches. End with step 2 on the third apartment.

5. Pick up an 8º, a blue cylinder, an orange cylinder, a drop bead, and a blue cylinder. Skip the blue cylinder, and pass your needle back up through the drop bead. Continue through the orange and blue cylinders. Pick up one 8º, one blue cylinder, one 8º, and one blue cylinder, and go through the 8º wall bead (**photo d**).

6. Pick up one orange cylinder and pass your needle through the bottom wall bead on the opposite side (**photo e**).

7. Repeat steps 3 and 2 until you have completed three more daisies. Then, repeat steps 5 and 6 to add the next dangle.

8. Continue working the pattern until you reach the length you like, then finish the necklace as desired. I used a large pressed-glass bead and made a peyote stitch loop for that bead to slip through. It blends in well with the necklace.

Looking for a more demure style? Try making a necklace with metallic seed beads and pearls. I used double-drilled pearls here, but the concept is the same. You can make the strap entirely of seed beads, or you can make pearl daisies to dress it up even more.

MULTILAYERED DAISY CHAIN

Daisy chains are great fun, but a field of daisies is even better. Start with a circle of daisy chain and then add as many layers as you like. This stitch works with all the different variations on basic daisy chain; you can have daisies that share walls, daisies that stand alone, traditional six-bead daisies, or daisies with as many beads around the centers as you like. The easiest way to learn this variation is to make a ring. Creating the first endless circle of daisy chain puts you in the right position to start the next row without having to weave through the beads to get into place.

MATERIALS:
- Japanese cylinder beads
- beading thread
- size 10 or 12 beading needle

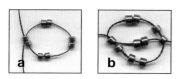

starting row 2

PROJECT

Ring of Daisies

We all have our runaway trains of thought. One idea leads to another and then to another. Sometimes the brain moves faster than the hands could ever hope to. My train of thought for this ring went something like this: … daisy chain … beads … tiny beads … pearls … tiny pearls … really tiny pearls … necklace … no, not yet … tiny beads … 15º beads … daisy chain … single layer … no, double … no, triple layer … RING! … I think I'll try it without pearls first … Go!

The first ring I made was a triple layer ring using nickel-colored Japanese cylinder beads, but as you can see, I've done it in a variety of colors and even with bead soup.

1. Pick up eight beads. Go back through the first bead to create a circle. You will have two beads for each wall, floor, and ceiling (**photo a**).

2. Pick up two beads, and pass your needle through the bottom wall bead on the opposite side (**photo b**).

3. Pick up six beads. Create a circle by passing your needle though the top wall bead above the bead your needle is exiting (**photo c**).

4. Repeat steps 2 and 3 until the chain almost fits around your finger. You will be creating a circle with this chain by adding just a tiny bit more to the circumference.

5. The wall on each end of the chain will form the walls of the last daisy, so you will need to add just a floor and a ceiling. Pick up two beads and pass your needle through the two wall beads of the other side (**photo d**).

6. Pick up two beads and pass your needle through the top wall bead to make the ceiling (**photo e**).

7. Pick up two beads and go through the bottom wall bead on the opposite side (**photo f**). You've created the first layer, an endless ring of daisies.

Be sure to keep good tension for the second (and third) layer of this ring.

8. Tie one or two tiny knots between the bead you are coming out of and the floor bead. Pass your needle through the two floor beads (**photo g**). These will now become the ceiling beads for this next layer.

9. Pick up six beads. Pass your needle through both ceiling beads and down the top wall bead (**photo h**).

10. Pick up two beads and go through the bottom wall bead on the opposite side to finish this stitch (**photo i**).

11. For the next stitch, you already have the ceiling and one wall. You will need to build only the floor and the other wall. Pick up four beads. Pass your needle through the two ceiling beads and down the top wall bead to complete the circle (**photo j**).

12. Repeat steps 10 and 11 until you've worked your way around the ring.

13. When you reach the last stitch, you will see that you already have the walls and the ceiling (**photo k**), so you need to add only the floor and the middle. Pick up two beads and go up the opposite wall, across the ceiling, and down the top wall bead (**photo l**).

14. Pick up two beads and pass your needle through the bottom wall bead on the opposite side (**photo m**).

To create another layer, repeat steps 8 through 14. Otherwise, weave in the tails, and trim the thread. Enjoy the ring!

I've had a lot of fun making this three-level ring with pearls in the center of the daisies. This is one of my very favorite creations - I get stopped on the street with this design! Make it like the "Ring of Daisies," but add beads where needed to fit around the pearls. I've also made rings that began with a circle of stand-alone daisies. The second layer of the ring is also made of stand-alone daisies, and shares only one bead (the ceiling/floor bead) with the row above, making the daisies look distinct and separate. When you use larger beads in the center of the daisies, you'll have beads in the corners that won't be part of the walls, floors, or ceilings. Leaving these beads unjoined, so that they ring only one daisy, can give the ring a lacy look or full look, depending on the size of the center bead.

When you use pearls in rings, try to find pearls that are as round as possible. Also, I don't recommend using glass pearls for this project, as the coating will wear off as you wear the ring.

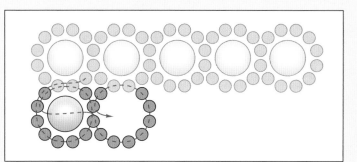

ALTERNATING DAISY CHAIN

You can change the look of daisy chain by moving the inside of the daisy to one of the edges. Instead of filling the center, a pearl could become a wall or ceiling. I love using this stitch with steel gray seed beads and creamy white freshwater pearls. The trick is to choose seed beads and accent beads that are proportionate – the accent bead should be about the same length as two seed beads.

Pick up two seed beads, one accent bead (a pearl), and four seed beads. Go back through the first bead you picked up, the top wall bead on the left.

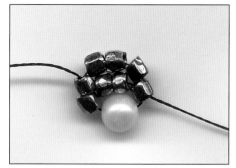

Pick up two seed beads and pass your needle through the bottom wall bead on the opposite side.

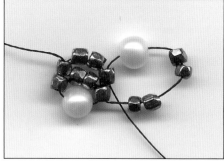

Pick up four seed beads and one accent bead. The seed beads will form the floor and a wall, and the accent bead will become the ceiling. Create a circle by passing your needle down through the adjoining top wall bead.

Pick up two seed beads and pass your needle through the bottom wall bead on the opposite side.

Pick up one accent bead and four seed beads and create a circle by passing your needle down through the adjoining top wall bead.

Continue until you reach your desired length.

Alternating ideas

You don't have to stick with
round beads for your alternating
accents. Try gemstone rondelles,
like the beautiful tanzanite beads
in this pair of earrings (above).

Alternating daisy chain also
can be used for multiple rows.
Check out the great pattern in
this ring (below).

Bead Play:
Peyote and daisy combined

The versatile daisy stitch is a perfect spacer between small sections of peyote stitch. In this project, the round black onyx beads are a classy complement to the nickel-colored 15º seed beads.

a

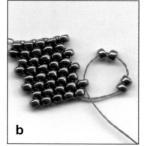

b

c

d

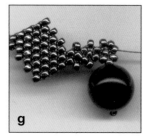

e

f

g

h

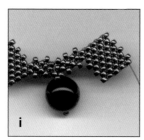

i

PROJECT

Graphic Necklace with Patches and Drops

1. Begin with a patch of even-count peyote (see Chapter 1) that is eight columns wide stitched for ten rows (**photo a**).

2. Notice the bead that your needle is exiting. This bead will be the bottom wall bead for the daisy chain stitch you are about to do. The bead right above this is the top wall bead. Pick up four beads. Create a circle by passing your needle back down into the aforementioned top wall bead (**photo b**).

3. Pick up one bead to fill in the center of the daisy stitch. Secure the bead by passing your needle down into the bottom wall bead on the opposite side (**photo c**).

4. Repeat steps 2 and 3 to make a second daisy (**photo d**).

5. Now add an onyx dangle. Pick up two seed beads, one onyx bead, and one seed bead. Skip the last seed bead, and go back up through the onyx bead and the next seed bead (**photo e**).

6. Pick up four seed beads. Create a circle by passing your needle down the top wall bead (**photo f**).

7. Pick up a seed bead to fill the center of the stitch, and go down through the bottom wall bead on the right (**photo g**).

8. Repeat steps 2–4.

9. The two wall beads of the last daisy stitch are the first two beads you will use for the next peyote patch. With your needle coming out of the bottom wall bead, pick up six beads (**photo h**).

10. Work peyote for 10 rows (**photo i**).

11. Repeat steps 2–10 until you have reached your desired length. Finish as desired. I used a peyote stitch toggle-and-loop closure.

> **MATERIALS:**
> - 15º seed beads, nickel
> - 6mm round gemstone beads, onyx
> - beading thread
> - size 10 or 12 beading needle

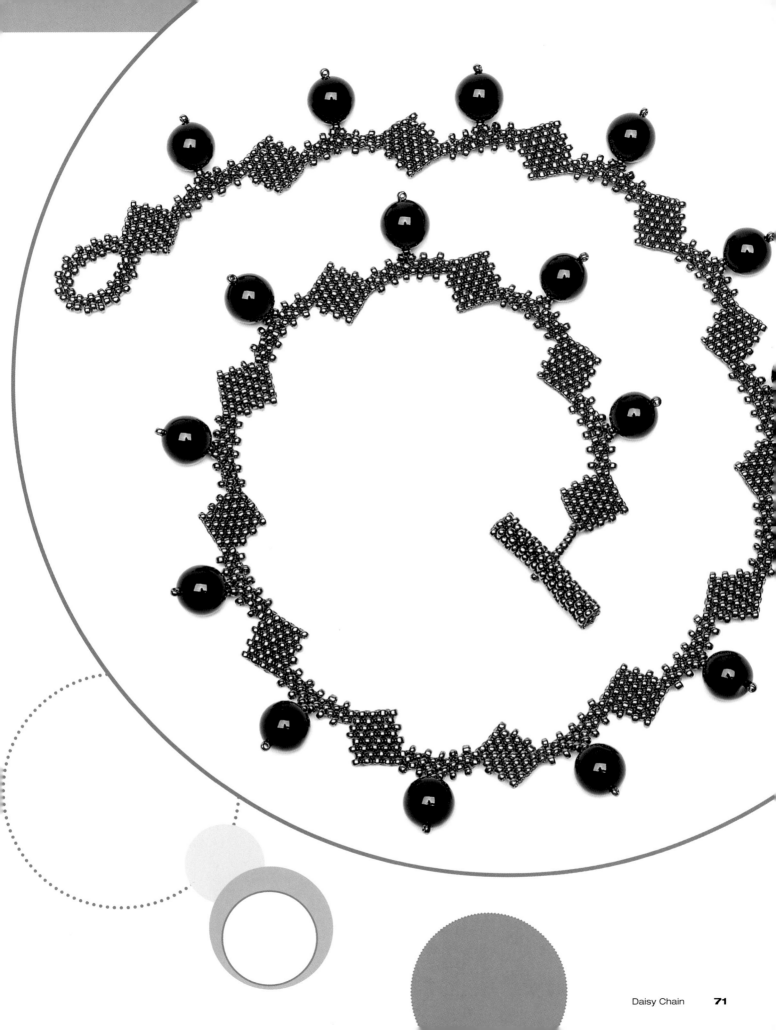

chapter 6

Spiral Rope Stitch

The spiral rope stitch creates a flexible and versatile twisting bead rope. Whether you go monochromatic or colorful, complex or simple, you get a great texture. Like all of the other stitches I have presented so far, you can create hundreds of different looks and textures depending on the beads you choose.

 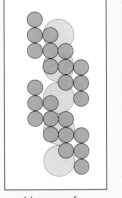 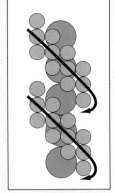 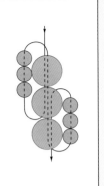 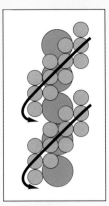

Spiral rope has a core of beads on the inside ...	and loops of different beads that spiral around the core.	You add the spiral one loop at a time by going back through the core beads several times, and passing through each loop of the spiral only once.	Always add each new loop to the same side of your last stitch. Your beadwork can spiral clockwise ...	or counterclockwise.

The type of spiral you'll get is determined by the amount of tension within the beadwork. If the loop of outer beads is shorter than the core beads it's spanning, the high tension will cause the core to spiral in conjunction with the outer beads.

If the loop of outer beads is longer than the core beads it is spanning, the low tension will allow the core to stay relatively straight, and the outer beads will spiral loosely around the core, as in the Sierra spiral, p. 76.

BASIC SPIRAL STITCH

Spiral stitch is a great opportunity to play with texture and color. Just remember, always pass your needle through the outer beads once and the core beads several times. Make sure the beads you choose for the core will be able to take four passes of thread. As you stitch, you'll notice that the outer beads from the new stitch are always a bit higher than the outer beads from the previous stitch. Make sure you are spiraling in a consistent direction.

Pick up four seed beads in color A and three seed beads in color B. Go through the color A beads again in the same direction.

Pick up a color A and three color Bs.

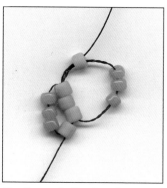

Go through the top four core beads: three color As from the first stitch and the color A you just picked up. Move the loop of Bs to sit next to the loop made in the previous stitch.

Pick up a new color A and three color Bs. Go through the top four core beads as before, and move the loop of Bs to sit beside the previous loops. Keep going until you reach the desired length.

Spiral variations

As I've said, there are plenty of ways to change this stitch by varying your bead and color choices. Here are some of my favorites.

One bead type – with pearls

Use small top-drilled pearls to create this dramatic effect. Begin regular spiral stitch by picking up seven beads (I used metallic hex-cuts with a multihued, or iris, finish) and going back through the four core beads. Pick up four beads and go back through the last three core beads and the first bead you picked up. (The tricky part of a single-bead rope is remembering which beads to go through again!) On the next stitch, pick up two hex-cuts, a pearl, and a hex-cut. Alternate regular hex-cut and pearl stitches until you reach the desired length. I finished this bracelet with a length of regular spiral stitch and secured it into a loop. Instead of my usual beaded toggle, I made a layered peyote stitch button.

Color block spiral stitch

It seems impossible for me to do this stitch in just one or two colors. I love to experiment with different bead colors and types to create interesting color blocks.

You may need to make adjustments when working with beads of different sizes. Using core beads that are smaller than your outer beads means that you may need to use two outer beads for each stitch instead of three as described above. If you are using outer beads that are smaller than your core beads, you may need to use more than three outer beads per stitch.

I'm often asked how I come up with color schemes for my work. Most of the time the ideas just happen, but the idea for this necklace (right) was born from some yarn my daughter used to make a hat and scarf. I found that the black beads made a nice backdrop for these autumn-hued colors. I used four 11º black core beads and three 11º green beads for the first stitch, then picked up one black and three green for the next ten stitches.

When I switched to the 6º yellow beads, I still picked up one core bead and three outer beads, but I did only five rows with the large beads. I switched back and forth between ten rows of 11ºs and five rows of 6ºs for the length of the necklace.

I made the color-blocked metallic necklace (below) using an assortment of beads in different shapes and sizes, including 11ºs, 8ºs, triangles, hex-cuts, cubes, and cylinder beads. I used four 15º beads for the core for each stitch.

SIERRA SPIRAL VARIATION

My younger daughter, Sierra, designed this spiral using four different kinds of beads. One bead type is used for the core, while the other three bead types are alternated for each stitch. You'll notice that the spirals around the core are relatively loose in this variation, allowing the core beads to sit in a straighter line.

PROJECT

Sierra Spiral Bracelet

This bracelet plays with the shape, finish, and color of the beads, which range from sharp-edged matte cubes to shiny pink-lined triangles to metallic 8º seed beads.

1. Pick up four 11ºs and three 8ºs. Circle back through the four 11ºs (**photo a**).

2. Pick up one 11º and two cube beads. Circle back through the top three 11ºs from the last stitch and the new 11º from this stitch (**photo b**).

3. Pick up an 11º and two 10º triangle beads. Circle back through the top three 11ºs from the last stitch and the new 11º from this stitch.

4. Continue working spiral stitch, alternating 8ºs, cubes, and triangles for each stitch (**photo c**). Work until you reach your desired length, then finish as desired. I sewed half of a sterling silver toggle clasp to each end of this bracelet.

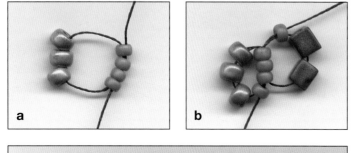

a

b

c

MATERIALS:
- 11º seed beads
- 8º seed beads
- 10º triangle beads
- 3–4mm cube beads
- beading thread
- size 10 or 12 beading needle

Sierra variations

As with regular spiral, you'll find plenty of ways to recreate and reimagine Sierra Spiral by changing the color, size, or amount of beads you're using.

Color play

Don't be afraid to step outside your normal color palette. Here I used a variety of bright pastels in three different sizes. Using mostly matte beads keeps the design from getting too busy, but the bright shades make it a standout.

The more, the merrier

You can use as many or as few beads as you wish to create the Sierra Spiral. This bracelet uses one bead for the core and seven different types of beads for the spiral.

Bead Play:
Advanced spiral

I love spiral patterns, so I wanted to get this one into the book. This lovely sculpted spiral, commonly known as Dutch Spiral, isn't related to the spiral rope stitch at all – in fact, it's a variation of tubular peyote stitch. But the loops of beads going around the rope reminded me of spiral rope stitch, so I put it here. You can make bracelets and necklaces or make small sections to be spaced with other beads.

MATERIALS:
- 11º seed beads, color A (green)
- 11º seed beads, color B (pink)
- 8º seed beads
- beading thread
- size 10 or 12 beading needle

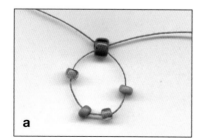

a

PROJECT
Sculpted Spiral Bracelet

1. Pick up five beads in this order: an 8º, a green 11º, a pink 11º, a green 11º, and a pink 11º. Circle back through the 8º (**photo a**).

2. Pick up a green 11º and go through the next green 11º (**photo b**).

3. Pick up a pink 11º and go through the next pink 11º (**photo c**).

4. Pick up a green 11º and go through the next green 11º (**photo d**). Notice that for steps 2–4, the color of the bead you picked up was the same as the color of the next bead you went through.

5. Pick up a green 11º, a pink 11º, and an 8º. Skip the last pink 11º, and go through the next 8º (the very first bead) to secure (**photo e**).

6. Repeat steps 2–4.

7. Pick up two green 11ºs, a pink 11º, and an 8º. Go through the next 8º (from step 5, see **photo f**).

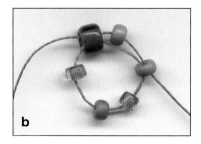
b

8. Repeat steps 2–4. Keep the tension tight, so that the beads start to form a tube.

9. Pick up three green 11ºs, a pink 11º, and an 8º, and go through the 8º from step 7.

10. Repeat steps 2–4.

c

11. Pick up four green 11ºs, a pink 11º, and an 8º. Go through the 8º from step 9.

12. Repeat steps 2–4.

13. Pick up five green 11ºs, a pink 11º, and an 8º. Go through the 8º from step 11. By now you've probably noticed that you're repeating the same two steps with an increase of one bead each time.

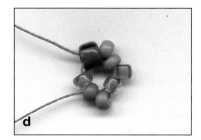
d

14. Repeat steps 2–4.

15. Pick up six green 11ºs, a pink 11º, and an 8º, and go through the next 8º. Repeat steps 2–4.

16. Now it's time to decrease. Repeat steps 13–14. Repeat again, this time picking up four green 11ºs. Continue repeating, decreasing one green 11º each time, until you are back to picking up one green 11º.

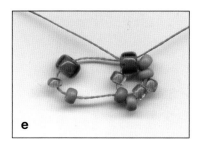
e

17. Repeat steps 2–16 until you reach the desired length. Finish as you'd like. I used a peyote stitch loop-and-toggle clasp.

f

For a little extra zing, try using use more than one color for the increased/decreased beads. In this example, I used 11ºs in black, white, and dark red, and 6ºs in mustard yellow. For the first part of the spiral, I alternated the black and white beads for each increase/decrease. For the second part of the spiral, I alternated the black and white beads within each increase/decrease. The effects are very different.

Russian Stitches

chapter 7

Russian Spiral, Fabulous Russian Rope, and St. Petersburg Chain are stitches I was inspired to learn when I saw some beautiful Russian beadwork. These three distinct stitches may not seem to have much in common, but they each represent a different approach to beading. I really wanted to learn the stitches, so I did some research on the Internet and got a copy of an elusive book known as the "white cover" Russian beadwork book; the book is written entirely in Russian, but has great illustrations and photographs. As usual, I've experimented with the stitches, and I'm excited to share with you what I've learned and discovered.

Russian Spiral

Russian spiral creates a hollow, lacy rope of beads. The best part? The different sizes and colors used in this stitch form a continuous spiral pattern around the rope. It's a thicker tube than most bead stitches, so it's great for bold colors and patterns.

Fabulous Russian Rope

This unusual rope stitch has the same basic end result as tubular right-angle weave, but it builds up in an unusual way. You will stitch several rows at once, and each row depends on the next to pull it into position. If you look at this stitch from the side, you can see that each row of beads sits in a different plane from the last row. In one row, the beads will sit horizontally, in the next they'll sit vertically.

St. Petersburg Chain

This is a great stitch for working with beads of different sizes. With a little experimentation, you can get distinctly different looks with identical bead combinations, depending on whether you put your accent beads on the outside edges ...

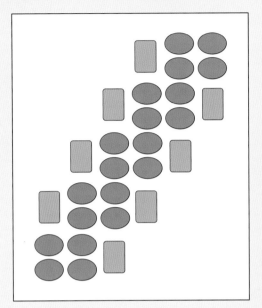

or in the center of each stitch.

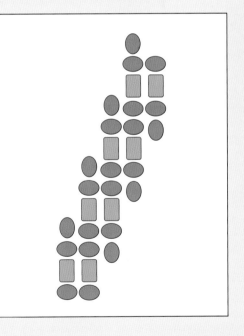

As you can see, this stitch moves naturally on the diagonal, so it's not surprising that I like it!

RUSSIAN SPIRAL

This stitch is a lot of fun, especially if you like to be creative with your color combinations. Though this stitch is a simple three-bead tubular netting stitch, the Russian variation uses two (or more) different sizes of beads to create a striking spiral effect. The basics of this stitch are easy to learn, and there is plenty of room for embellishment.

Start by stringing nine beads in this order: two 11ºs, one 8º, two 11ºs, one 8º, two 11ºs, and one 8º. Create a circle of beads by going through all the beads again. Continue through the first bead, an 11º, a third time. Make sure that you always bead in the same direction. (I bead in a counterclockwise motion.)

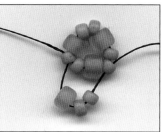

Pick up an 8º and two 11ºs. Skip the next 11º and 8º on the ring, and go through the following 11º. As you're beading, you will always go through the 11º after the next 8º.

Pick up an 8º and two 11ºs, and go through the first 11º after the next 8º, as before.

Continue around the same way. When you finish the row, your thread will come out the same bead the tail is exiting.

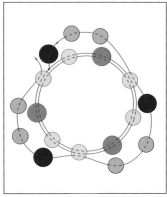

The row you just completed is the second row of the beaded rope. As you stitch, gently pull the beads into a tube shape. To get ready to begin round 3, you will need to do a step-up, which you will do at the end of every row.

To step up, pass your needle through the 8º and the first 11º that you added in the first stitch of the round.

To begin the next row, pick up one 8º and two 11ºs. Skip the next 11º and 8º and go through the following 11º. As on the previous row, you'll always pass your needle through the 11º after the next 8º you come to.

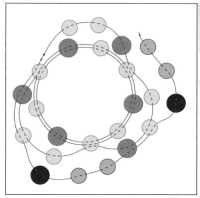

Continue around, then step up to start the next round as before. You may notice that when you step up to start the next row, the 11º is a tiny bit lower than the next beads. That's okay!

To count the rows, start at the end of the rope and count the 8ºs spiraling around the tube. You are not counting every 8º in the tube, just one spiral of them.

Russian spiral variations

The variation possibilities are endless depending on the beads you use — you can use two or three different beads. I don't recommend using just one type of bead as you may quickly lose your place.

Change size or color

Try following the instructions, but replacing one of the 11°s with a different color bead, or a 15°. I had a lot of fun experimenting as I created this necklace, and I love the way the different bead combinations change the thickness of the tube.

Add a surface embellishment

For the necklace at right, I added a picot embellishment (see p. 29) to the first bead added to every stitch for the last five rows of each color section. The texture becomes part of the color pattern, and the picots emphasize the spiral.

For the necklace made with black, white, and red beads (above), I added the picot only to the first bead of each new row. This allows the red to spiral around the rope.

FABULOUS RUSSIAN ROPE

When I taught myself how to do this stitch my first thought was, "Wow, this is fabulous." I guess the name stuck for me because that is what I call this technique. I don't know of any other name. The boxy shape of this rope lends itself beautifully to patterns and color blocking. The original instructions from which I learned this stitch have the beader changing direction every row. After reading my instructions, Lynne Irelan suggested a way to do this stitch without having to change direction. The end result is the same. This stitch has proven to be a bit tricky in a couple of my classes and may take a few attempts (as well as some patience) to get the hang of it.

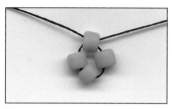

You can use any number of bead sizes, colors or shapes. For these instructions, I will be using three colors to help you keep track of the rows. To make things easy, I'll call them what they are: blue, orange, and yellow.

Pick up four blue beads and create a circle by going back through the first bead. This is row 1.

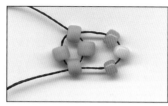

With your needle coming out of the first blue bead, pick up three beads: one orange, one yellow, and one orange. Skip over the next blue bead, and go through the third blue bead. Notice that you are passing your needle through the bead directly opposite the first bead.

Pick up one orange, one yellow, and one orange. Skip the fourth blue bead and pass your needle into the first blue bead again.

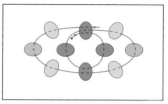

What you have just created is the first two-and-a-half rows of the rope. The four blue beads make up the first row, the four orange beads make up the second row, and the two yellow beads make up half of the third row. Right now these rows look flat, but once you complete the third row, the orange and yellow beads will pull up into place.

Now you'll step up to complete the third row. Your thread is coming out of the first blue bead. Go through the next orange bead and the yellow bead. Pull up the beads so the yellow beads are across from each other, with no beads between them.

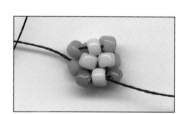

Pick up a yellow bead and pass your needle through the next yellow bead. Pick up one more yellow bead and go into the first yellow bead. The yellow row now has four sides.

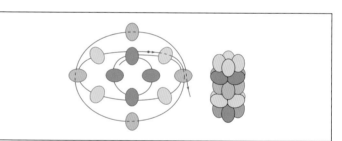

Now you'll pick up the beads for rows 4 and 5 just like you did for rows 2 and 3. (The yellow row is now the base row, like the blue row you started with.) Pick up one blue bead, one orange bead, and one blue bead. Skip a yellow bead and go through the following yellow bead, opposite where you started. Pick up a blue bead, an orange bead, and a blue bead, and go through the first yellow bead again.

The four blue beads that were picked up in these two steps make up the beads for row 4. The two orange beads make up two of the four beads for row 5.

Step up to come out of an orange bead, pick up an orange bead, and go through the opposite orange bead. Pick up an orange bead, and go through the first orange bead. Pull the beads into the tube shape. The orange beads now act as the base row. Continue on as before, adding three beads to each side, then stepping up to complete the row.

Fabulous Russian rope variations

I love using this stitch with beads of all colors, but the boxy structure really helps simple patterns stand out as well. Time to get out the beads and play.

Simple pattern with pearls

Bronze seed beads are a nice contrast to these little creamy white freshwater pearls. I worked the first section of the rope with bronze seed beads, then added pearl accents at regular intervals. To make the pearl flowers, I started by picking up a pearl, a seed bead, and a pearl for the three-bead sequence. After the step-up, I picked up a pearl for each one-bead stitch. To complete the flower, I picked up a pearl, a seed bead, and a pearl for the next three-bead sequence, did the step-up, and picked up a seed bead for each one-bead stitch. Then I resumed stitching the bronze seed bead pattern.

Color and bead fun

Every summer my daughters go to overnight camp for three weeks, and every summer I make them some type of beaded bracelet that represents the messages "miss you" and "love you." The phrases "miss you" and "love you" each have seven letters. This past summer I made them each a bracelet that I called "rope bracelet with a secret" (right). The secret was that one of the beads in the bracelet is used seven times to represent the letters in "miss you" and "love you." They loved trying to figure out the secret, and I loved the opportunity to have fun with my bead choices.

This stitch is so much fun to play with. For the necklace (left), I experimented with different patterns. I color blocked and I made little "flower" patterns and stripes. I added a freeform toggle clasp in the shape of a heart so that the necklace can be worn with an optional pendant look.

ST. PETERSBURG CHAIN

This flexible stepped chain works great with dangles and curves gracefully in necklaces and bracelets. The chain might look a little complicated, but it's easy to learn. Fitting the different types and sizes of beads together is like putting together a puzzle – some pieces fit together, and some don't. While you can use almost any type of bead, I recommend using the same beads as I do while you're learning this stitch and its variations.

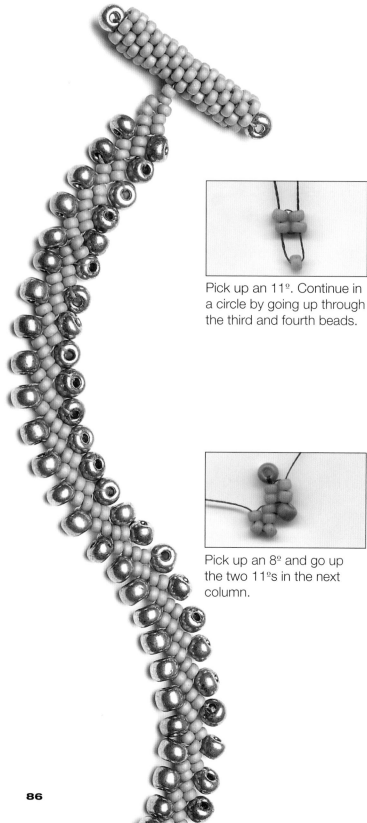

Start by picking up four 11º beads. Go through the first two beads again in the same direction.

Pick up an 11º. Continue in a circle by going up through the third and fourth beads.

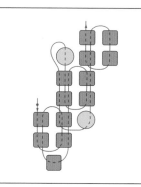

Pick up four 11ºs, and go through the sixth and seventh beads again in the same direction to make a circle. These four beads are not attached to the last segment yet, so make sure to push the beads tight to the beadwork so that you have no unwanted gaps.

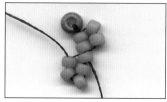

Pick up an 8º, turn, and go back down the next three 11ºs in the column. This joins the two segments.

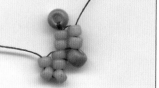

Pick up an 8º and go up the two 11ºs in the next column.

Pick up four 11ºs and go through the first two of these beads again to form a circle.

Like the last segment, these beads aren't joined to the chain yet, so pull the circle tight to the previous segment.

Continue adding the 8ºs as you did for the last segment. You can use this as a sample or continue beading to make a bracelet like mine or a necklace.

St. Petersburg variations

It is amazing how much this stitch can change if you just play with bead shapes and sizes. Unlike most of the other stitches in this book, changing the beads you use in St. Petersburg chain will usually change the bead count, too. Some beads fit together better than others. I've played around with this stitch quite a bit, and here are some of my favorite bead variations. Once you're well acquainted with the stitch, why don't you see what you can come up with?

PROJECT

Metallic Chain with Pearls

In case you haven't figured it out, I love steel gray combined with creamy white pearls. When I found these wonderful twisted 8º hex-cut Japanese cylinder beads, I knew there was a necklace in their future. Working in St. Petersburg chain, I combined the larger hex-cuts with smaller hex-cuts. Large pearls spaced evenly throughout the necklace heightens the drama.

Before beginning these instructions, look back at the pictures for the basic St. Petersburg chain. You will see that each stitch has two pairs of beads lined up side by side, forming stacks or columns. The pattern for this necklace uses three-bead stacks. Look back at p. 86, and you'll see that I used four beads for the initial circle of each segment. For this necklace, you will pick up six beads for the initial circles. It's useful to think of these beads as two stacks. Each stack will have one small hex-cut, one large hex-cut, and one small hex-cut.

1. Pick up six beads in this order: one small hex-cut, one large hex-cut, two small hex-cuts, one large hex-cut, and one small hex-cut. Create a circle of beads by passing your needle back through the first three beads you strung, the first small, large, small stack of hex-cuts (**photo a**).

2. Pick up a small hex-cut, and continue around the circle, passing your needle up through the next three beads (**photo b**).

3. Pick up one small hex-cut, one large hex-cut, two small hex-cuts, one large hex-cut, and one small hex-cut. Create another circle of beads by passing your beads through the first three beads just strung (**photo c**). Remember, these beads aren't really attached to the last section of beadwork, so pull the circle tight to the beadwork.

4. Notice the bead stack that your thread is exiting. Pick up one small hex-cut, turn, pass your needle back down the same three-bead stack, and continue into the first small hex-cut in the stack below (**photo d**).

5. Pick up a small hex-cut, and pass your needle up into the next stack of three beads in the new circle (**photo e**).

6. Repeat this pattern, making a circle with two stacks of three beads and picking up the two small hex-cuts, until you have completed five segments (**photo f**).

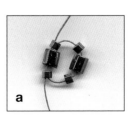

a

b

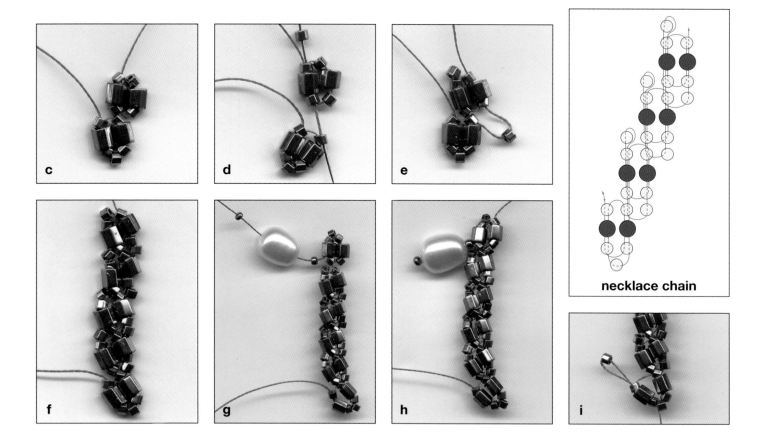

c

d

e

f

g

h

necklace chain

i

MATERIALS:
- 8º twisted hex-cut Japanese cylinder beads
- 12º twisted hex-cut Japanese cylinder beads
- 15º seed beads
- 12mm freshwater pearls, drilled top-to-bottom
- beading thread
- size 10 or 12 beading needle

7. Make the next circle of beads. Pick up the first small hex-cut, turn, and go back through the small hex-cut and the large hex-cut. Pick up a 15º bead, a pearl, and a 15º (**photo g**).

8. Skip the last 15º, and go back up through the pearl and the first 15º. Go through the last small hex-cut of the stack and into the first small hex-cut of the next stack. Pick up a small hex-cut, and finish the segment as usual (**photo h**).

9. Continue stitching, creating segments and adding pearl dangles as desired. I added a pearl dangle to every sixth segment. Finish the end as desired. I made a peyote toggle-and-loop clasp.

Notice that your initial tail thread is coming out of a small hex-cut at the top of the three bead stack in the first segment. Pick up one small hex-cut, and pass your needle down through that same three-bead stack. You are now in position to finish the end as desired (**photo i**).

Once you're familiar with the pattern of the stitch, you can use whatever beads you like in any pattern or mix you prefer. As you can probably guess by now, I like to use bead soup.

PROJECT

Three Bracelets with Bugle Beads

These three bracelets follow the same pattern, but two use seed beads (8ºs and 11ºs) instead of the cube beads called for in the following instructions. This pattern is very close to the hex-cut variation – only the beads are different.

1. Pick up one cube bead, one bugle bead, two cubes, one bugle, and one cube. Circle back through the first three beads – one cube, one bugle, and one cube. These are the first two stacks of your first segment (**photo a**).

2. Pick up one cube, and continue through the last three beads – one cube, one bugle, and one cube (**photo b**).

3. Pick up one cube, one bugle, two cubes, one bugle, and one cube. Circle back through the first three beads you just strung – one cube, one bugle, and one cube (**photo c**). (I purposely showed the two circles of beads as being separate, but be sure that you push the beads tightly together to close the gap.)

4. Pick up one cube, turn, and go back down through the three beads in the new stack (cube, bugle, cube) and the first cube in the previous stack (**photo d**).

5. Pick up one cube bead. Pass your needle up through the next cube-bugle-cube stack in the new segment (**photo e**).

6. Pick up one cube, one bugle, two cubes, one bugle, and one cube, and make the next segment as you did the last one. Continue adding segments until you reach the desired length.

7. You should have two three-bead rows of cubes except at the beginning of the bracelet. To finish the piece, use the starting tail to pick up a cube. Turn, and pass your needle down through the three beads in the column (**photo f**). Now you are ready to add the clasp of your choice to each end of the bracelet. I chose a simple spring clasp.

MATERIALS
- 3–6mm bugle beads
- cube beads or 8º or 11º seed beads
- beading thread
- size 10 or 12 beading needle

a

b

c

d

e

f

Bead Play:
Sampler necklaces and pendants

Sometimes my attention span resembles that of a 2-year-old. I actually surprise myself when I complete a necklace or a bracelet that uses only one stitch. What I really like is to start with one stitch for a few rows and then switch to another, then another, and then another. This process turned out a series of necklaces I call "samplers" – a perfect name for showing samples of many different stitches using many different bead colors and types. Who could get bored making one, two, or more of these?

To begin the sampler necklaces, I usually start with a small patch of peyote stitch, and continue with small sections of any of the other stitches I know. When moving from one stitch to the next, make sure to use the last bead of one section as the first bead of the next section. This will keep the sections together, and you will avoid having any gaps in your work.

This sampler necklace was one of the first I ever made. I chose to use muted shades accented with red and combined peyote with tri stitch, brick stitch, and peyote twists.

Incorporating new and vintage glass beads added a bold accent to this fun necklace.

Making a pendant (opposite page, left) is a little different, but the concept is the same. I started with a simple sampler bracelet, finished with a beaded toggle clasp. When I was done, I held it in my hands and started twisting it.

I pushed the toggle through the loop at the bottom of the twist, and, before I knew it, I had a folded freeform pendant in my hand. I made a neck strap using my signature style of alternating seed beads with a loop in the middle, and attached the pendant toggle to the loop.

Cool, don't you think? You will create a new look every time you twist it. Be careful not to stress the thread too much as you are twisting.

I have a lot of fun using peyote twists (remember those, from Bead Play, Chapter 1?). These two necklaces use similar colors, but the stitches used in each are different.

What is it about black and white that looks so amazing when paired with brightly colored beads? This necklace uses elements of Russian spiral, spiral rope, and daisy chain along with other basic stitches. I finished the necklace with a more elaborate toggle clasp.

Final thoughts

Somebody once said that "a stranger is a friend you have not yet met." My personal bead journey is very much like that. A stitch I did not know or know how to master yesterday is one of my favorite bead stitches today or may become my favorite tomorrow. I like to introduce myself to new ideas all the time, and that's the purpose of this book – introducing you to new ideas. If you are a beginning beader, I hope you've been excited by new stitches. Please keep in mind as you are learning that I did not pick up a needle, thread, and beads and make a sampler necklace. I first had to learn the basics, just like you will. While I am fortunate that beading comes very easily to me, I did have a few moments of frustration along the way, and I know that it does not come easily to everyone. All beaders learn differently. Some read books, some take classes, some use color wheels. Some beaders follow a bead pattern exactly as written, while others just skim through to get the idea. No matter how you learn, the most important thing is to have fun. If you find that one stitch is more challenging than you had hoped, put it down and try a different one. There is no right or wrong in the world of bead stitching. Once you master the concept of a stitch, find a way to take it in a new direction and make it your own. For seasoned beaders as well as beginning beaders, if I have inspired you in even the smallest way, then I have succeeded in what I set out to do.

Throughout this book I have shown you just a small sampling of all of the bead choices available today. I have also used several of my favorite color and texture combinations. Now it is your turn to find colors and textures that you like and to create your own bead-stitched piece of art. Remember to play, have fun, and, most of all, share what you have learned. Please feel free to contact me with any questions. I always love to see what beaders have created using some of my ideas and techniques. I can be reached at bnshdl@msn.com or through my Web site, bethstone.com.

Remember my favorite bead class icebreaker question from the introduction? Beads or food? What is your choice? I think you know mine. Oh, and do you know what beads and chocolate have in common? They are both hard to resist!

Thank you for allowing me to share my love of beads with you.

Beth

Acknowledgments

I would like to thank the many people who have helped make this book possible:

- My very creative and loving mother, Ina Katz, for passing down the "beading" gene, and my late father, Sam Katz, for giving me my "math mind."

- All of the wonderful people at Kalmbach Publishing Co., especially Lesley Weiss, who trusted in this project from the beginning and worked hard to make it a reality. Pat Lantier, thank you for your constant encouragement and support. Mindy Brooks guided me for years from *Bead&Button* to *BeadStyle* and back to *Bead&Button*; thanks for the guidance here.

- The readers of *Bead&Button* and *BeadStyle* magazines who have shared their kind words and beautiful work with me through the years. Thank you for allowing me to inspire you.

- My friends. Thanks for cheering me on. Now I have time for lunch.

- Lynne Irelan and Cissy Gast. Although we have never met, I appreciate the time you have taken to test out my instructions, make corrections and suggestions, and just be there for me.

- Jeannette Cook. Thank you for allowing me to share your "apartment building" technique. It was just what I needed.

- Bobbe Kelley. Thanks for your help in testing the Pebble Stitch instructions.

- My amazing sister, Lori Silverstein. Laughter will get us through anything!

- And most importantly, my husband, Sheldon, and our two beautiful and creative daughters, Cheyenne and Sierra. I love you more than you know. I could not have taken on a project of this size without your love and support. Thank you for stepping over and around the bead mess. And remember, "a house is not a home unless you can write 'I love you' in the dust" (author unknown).

About Beth Stone

Beth Stone calls beadwork "a puzzle with infinite solutions."

The third in a line of beading artists — her grandmother was a beader and artist and her mother still is — Beth's first love is seed bead work and creating pieces of art by combining tiny points of color using different off-loom bead-stitching techniques. In addition to her seed bead work, she also creates one-of-a-kind and limited edition bracelets and necklaces using vintage and new glass, sterling silver, freshwater pearls, and gemstones. Completely self-taught, Beth says her mistakes are often the best lessons.

Beth has shown her work at local art shows since 1990 and had her work displayed and sold in a number of fine-art galleries and gift stores, most recently at the Birmingham Bloomfield Art Center in Birmingham, Mich. In 1998, one of her pieces was published in *Bead&Button* magazine; she calls its publication "a dream come true." Since then, many of her creations have been featured in the magazine. In addition, from the premiere issue until January 2006, Beth was one of the contributing editors for *BeadStyle* magazine. Her work can also be seen in various books and booklets from Kalmbach Publishing.

"Creativity is allowing yourself to make mistakes. Art is knowing which ones to keep."

– *Scott Adams*

No matter how you bead,
these books satisfy your need